SENSUOUS
SCHOLARSHIP

CONTEMPORARY ETHNOGRAPHY

Series Editors
DAN ROSE
PAUL STOLLER

A complete list of books in the series
is available from the publisher.

SENSUOUS

SCHOLARSHIP

PAUL STOLLER

University of Pennsylvania Press

Philadelphia

10 9 8 7 6 5 4 3 2 1

Published by
University of Pennsylvania Press
Philadelphia, Pennsylvania 19104-6097

Library of Congress Cataloging-in-Publication Data
Stoller, Paul
  Sensuous scholarship / Paul Stoller
    p.   cm. — (Contemporary Ethnography)
  Includes bibliographical references and index
  ISBN 0-8122-3398-0 (cloth : alk. paper). — ISBN 0-8122-1615-6
(pbk. : alk. paper)
  1. Ethnology—Methodology. 2. Ethnology—Philosophy.
3. Sensuality. 4. Songhai (African people)—Religion. 5. Sonhgai
(African people)—History. 6. Songhai (African people)—
Social conditions.
  I. Title. II. Series.
GN345.S45   1997   96-53514
305.8′001—dc21   CIP

Frontispiece: The Sensuous Word: Harouna Beidari (l) Accompanied
by Idrissa Souley, Recites Old Words, The Epic of Askia Mohammed,
at Karma, Niger May 9, 1981. Photo by Thomas A. Hale.

CONTENTS

Acknowledgments   vii

Prologue: The Scholar's Body   ix

Part One: Embodied Practices   1

Introduction: The Way of the Body   3

1. The Sorcerer's Body   4

2. The Griot's Tongue   24

Part Two: Body and Memory   45

Introduction: The Texture of Memory   47

3. Embodying Colonial Memories   48

4. "Conscious" Ain't Consciousness: Entering the Museum of Sensory Absence   74

Part Three: Embodied Representations   89

Introduction: Embodying the Grammar   91

5. Spaces, Places, and Fields: The Politics of West African Trading in New York City's Informal Economy   93

6. Artaud, Rouch, and the Cinema of Cruelty   119

Epilogue: Sensuous Ways of Knowing/Living   135

Notes   139

Works Cited   149

Films Cited   161

Index   163

ACKNOWLEDGMENTS

The paths authors follow from the conception, the gestation, and finally the birth of their books are rarely, if ever, solitary ones. More than most authors, anthropologists depend on a wide variety of people and institutions to support their research and writing. This book would have never come to life without the support, encouragement, and critical insight of a wide variety of friends and colleagues in the Republic of Niger, France, and the United States.

Whatever insights I may have gained as a scholar derive in large measure from ongoing field studies among Songhay-speaking people in Niger and New York City. For the past twenty years, my fieldwork has been generously supported by the National Endowment for the Humanities, the National Science Foundation, the Wenner-Gren Foundation for Anthropological Research, and West Chester University. I am also grateful for funds from the John Simon Guggenheim Memorial Foundation and the National Endowment for the Humanities and hospitality from the School of American Research, all of which provided time and space for reflection and writing. I thank the Government of Niger for granting me authorizations to conduct ethnographic research in Mehanna and Tillaberi in western Niger.

There are many people to thank for their direct and indirect contributions to this book. In Niger, the friendship of Diouldé Laya, Director of the Organization of African Unity's Center for Oral, Linguistic, and Historical Tradition, has been a source of great inspiration. The kindness and hospitality of Thomas Price, Hadiza Djibo, and the Djibo family have made my visits to Niger sparkle with good cheer and stimulating conversation — indispensable elements for the anthropologist in the field.

I have learned much about anthropology from the example of colleagues in France. Although we often disagree about social theories and ethnographic practices, the scholarly work of Marc Piault, Jean-Pierre Olivier de Sardan, Alice Sindzingre, Suzanne

Lallemand, Laurent Vidal, Edmond Bernus, the late Suzanne Bernus, the late Nicole Echard, and the late Jean-Marie Gibbal has been much appreciated. The example of Jean Rouch, *cinéaste extraordinaire,* has been an ongoing inspiration.

In North America many friends and colleagues have commented on various chapters of this book. For their constructively critical thoughts I thank T. David Brent, John Chernoff, Rosemary Coombe, Alan Feldman, Alma Gottlieb, Laura Graham, John Homiak, Kirin Narayan, Cheryl Olkes, Marina Roseman, C. Nadia Seremetakis, and Richard Waller. I am also thankful for the fine commentaries of Phil Kilbride and David Napier who read the manuscript for the University of Pennsylvania Press. Their insightful observations steered me in fruitful directions. I am grateful for Jasmin Tahmaseb McConatha's careful reading of the entire manuscript. Her comments have substantially improved the book. Patricia Smith of the University of Pennsylvania Press has patiently urged me to write this book. I hope the result of my labors meets her expectations.

* * *

Some of the material in this book has been revised from previously published works. A version of Chapter 2 appeared as "Ethnographies as Texts/Ethnographers as Griots," *American Ethnologist* 20 (2) (1993): 353–67. A version of Chapter 3 appeared under the same title in *American Anthropologist* 96 (3) (1994): 634–49. A version of Chapter 5 appeared under the same title in *American Anthropologist* 98 (4) (1996): 776–88. A version of Chapter 6 appeared under the same title in *Visual Anthropology Review* 8 (2) (1992): 50–58. All copyright © American Anthropological Association.

A version of Chapter 4 appeared in *The Senses Still: Perception and Memory as Material Culture,* ed. C. Nadia Serematakis. Boulder, Co.: Westview Press, 1994. Reprinted by permission of Westview Press.

The names of interviewees in chapter 5 have been changed.

PROLOGUE

The Scholar's Body

> We are the mirror
> as well as the face in it.
> We are tasting the taste this minute
> of eternity. We are the pain
> and what causes pain, both. We are the
> sweet, cold water and the jar that pours
> —Rumi

The thought of being "the sweet, cold water and the jar that pours" pushed the din of the coffee shop's early morning breakfast trade far into the background of my awareness. Immersed in mystical Sufi stories, I pondered mirrors and faces rather than omelettes and French toast, the real and the surreal rather than bagels and cream cheese.

"You look lost, old man."

I looked up from my book and smiled at my old friend David. I had returned to New York in July 1993 to continue field studies of West African peddlers on the streets of Harlem. David, also an anthropologist, and Mark, a filmmaker, had come to Manhattan to do a shoot. Because David's creative insights had always stimulated me, I had wanted him to see "the guys" on 125th Street. Perhaps his aesthetic intuitions might steer me in fruitful directions? We had arranged to meet for breakfast at the Excelsior Hotel coffee shop before going uptown. It promised to be a hot July day—prime time for a visit to the African market.

David and Mark sat down opposite me in the noisy coffee shop.

"I've been reading Sufi stories this summer," I said.

"Yeah, I've read some of those stories," David responded. "I like them, too."

Our waiter emerged from the coffee shop's early morning swirl.

"What you want?" he asked sharply in Polish accented English. "You want coffee? bagel? eggs?"

We sat in our booth somewhat numbed both by the earliness of the hour and the waiter's intensity.

"I get you coffee," he said without waiting for our reply. "Then I come back." He barked out an order for three coffees.

The waiter returned with our coffees. "Now what you want? Eggs? English muffin? Toast?" He rocked on his heels. "You ready?"

After we ordered, David reached over for the book of stories I had been reading. He looked at the cover and caressed the book's spine. "Let's try something."

"I'm ready," I answered, for David's playfulness often resulted in wonderfully creative ad hoc experiments.

"Good. Let's see what story I turn to?" He opened the book to the following story and read it to us.

*   *   *

Mojud was a moderately prosperous official in a Kingdom, who foresaw a promotion to Inspector of Weights and Measures. One day, however, Mojud saw the image of Khadir, the guide of the Sufis. Khadir told him to quit his job and present himself by the river's edge in three days' time. With much ambivalence, Mojud quit his very desirable job. His peers thought him crazy, but soon forgot about him. Three days passed and Mojud went to the river's edge where he saw Khadir, who ordered him to tear off his clothes and jump into the river. "We'll see if someone saves you."

Mojud dived into the river and was swept downstream. Since he knew how to swim, he didn't drown, but the river's current carried him a long way. Eventually, a fisherman scooped him out of the water.

The fisherman asked: "Why have you been in the river? You could drown."

"I'm not sure," said Mojud. Having pity for the hapless survivor, the fisherman took him in. Mojud learned how to fish and taught the fisherman how to read and write. After five months Khadir appeared again and ordered him to leave. Mojud left reluctantly and walked along a road, where he encountered a passing farmer who wondered if he desired work. Mojud said yes. In this way, he spent two years with the farmer, during which he amassed savings. Khadir again appeared and told him to leave the farmer and use his savings to become a skin merchant. Although he liked his life on the farm, he journeyed to Mosul, where he became a well-known trader. After he had saved quite a bit of money, Khadir came yet again. This time he demanded that Mojud give away all his money and travel to Samarkand, where he would work for a grocer. Not knowing what to expect, Mojud obeyed. In Samarkand Mojud began to show signs of spiritual illumination. He healed the sick and advised the wise. As time passed, increasing numbers of people, old and young, rich and poor, came to him for guidance. In this way, Mojud, now a great Sufi, founded the Naqshbandi Order.[1]

* * *

We discussed the story, and agreed that by following his heart and lending his body to the world Mojud received the great wisdom born of the fusion of heart and head. By linking head and heart Mojud forged rather than severed the interconnectedness of things, reinforcing the seamless fit of the intelligible and the sensible. We talked of how the sensuous wonders of the world had so humbled Mojud that he let them illuminate his being.

"This seems like a very good way to do anthropology," David said.

David's statement, based on his reaction to a randomly selected Sufi story, fired my thinking about this book. I had for some time wanted to write a volume about how experience-in-the-world might awaken a scholar's body. The awakening experience in the coffee shop compelled me to write what follows.

Reformulating the Body

Stiffened from long sleep in the background of scholarly life, the scholar's body yearns to exercise its muscles. Sleepy from long inactivity, it aches to restore its sensibilities. Adrift in a sea of half-lives, it wants to breathe in the pungent odors of social life, to run its palms over the jagged surface of social reality, to hear the wondrous symphonies of social experience, to see the sensuous shapes and colors that fill windows of consciousness. It wants to awaken the imagination and bring scholarship back to "the things themselves."[2]

Wants, however, are far from being deeds, for a sensuous awakening is a very tall order in an academy where mind has long been separated from body, sense long severed from sensibility. This scholarly disconnectedness is the very antithesis of Mojud's sensuous celebrations of life. What can his embodied example mean to fin de siècle scholars?

The body has long been an important locus in the discourse of the human sciences. In the seventeenth century, the rationalists believed the sensuous body an object to be distrusted, if not reviled, lest its subjectivities steer us away from objective perceptions. Such a longstanding conceit provoked much critical discourse along the side roads of social theory. One thinks immediately of Montaigne, Nietzsche, Husserl, and Heidegger —a diverse array of thinkers who critiqued classical rationalism. In his critique of Cartesianism, Maurice Merleau-Ponty focused on two primary myths: laws of nature and scientific explanation.

This rationalism seems so full of myths to us: the myth of *laws of nature* vaguely situated halfway between norms and facts, and *according to which*, it was thought, this nevertheless blind world has been constructed; the myth of *scientific explanation*, as if knowledge of relations, even extended to all observable phenomena, could one day transform the very existence of the world into an analytic and self-evident proposition. . . . Reason was confused with knowledge of conditions or causes: wherever a conditioning factor was discovered, it was thought that every question has been silenced, the problem of essence resolved along with the problem of origin, and the fact brought under the jurisdiction of its cause. . . . Each conquest made for determinism was a defeat for the metaphysical sense, whose victory necessarily involved the "failure of science."[3] (emphasis in original)

Although philosophers of science and social theorists have routinely criticized these classical myths, elements of them remain intact. Take, for example, the quest for disembodied observation, which in the "best of all possible worlds" (to evoke Voltaire) is transformed into disembodied representation, a bloodless prose that saps the body of its sensuousness.

For almost a generation, social theorists and cultural critics have questioned the classical supposition that rigorous research methods result in more or less objective observations. This criticism devolves primarily from two sources: feminism and poststructuralism. Feminists have discussed the epistemological and political ramifications of Cartesianism. They have demonstrated forcefully not only how science is misled by the inherent sexism of past and present Cartesianism, but also how the myths of science have been used to reinforce women's powerlessness.

Through the Cartesian "rebirth," a new "masculine" theory of knowledge is delivered, in which detachment from nature acquires a positive epistemological value. And a new *world* is reconstructed, one in which all generativity and creativity fall to God, the spiritual father, rather than to the female "flesh" of the world. With the same masterful stroke—the mutual opposition of the spiritual and the corporeal—the formerly female earth becomes inert matter and the objectivity of science is insured.[4] (emphasis in original)

Poststructuralists, for their part, have deconstructed the epistemology of rationalism, calling into question what John Dewey called "the quest for certainty." They have also shown how the state has used a variety of discourses to manipulate bodies. These strategies have enabled the state to maintain or, in some cases, increase its power over subject(ed) peoples.[5]

In cases like Emily Martin's study, *The Woman in the Body* (1987), poststructuralist and feminist approaches are combined. Martin demonstrates the social, cultural, and bodily consequences of an overtly sexist nosology based on the Cartesian separation of mind and body. But Martin is by no means a single embodied voice among anthropologists, sociologists, and other thinkers. Seeking to avoid the epistemological and political pitfalls of Cartesianism, a growing number of scholars have used the notion of the body—and embodiment—to criticize both Eurocentric and phallocentric predispositions in scholarly thought. As a result the sensuous body has recently emerged as a new site of analysis. Pierre Bourdieu writes:

Taste, a class culture turned into nature, that is embodied helps to shape the class body. It is an incorporated principle of classification which governs all forms of incorporation, choosing and modifying everything that the body ingests and digests and assimilates, physiologically and psychologically. It follows that the body is the most indisputable materialization of class taste.[6]

As Byran Turner points out, the body has a secret history in social theory, stemming from Nietzsche's Dionysian diversions into the erotics of the body, the sensuality of dance, and the rapture of ecstacy. Until recently, Turner argues, this secret history had been superfluous. "In recent developments of social theory, there has been an important reevaluation of the importance of the body, not simply in feminist social theory, but more generally in the analysis of class, culture and consumption."[7]

Much of the emerging social science writing on the body therefore centers on Western conceptions. The essays in Mike Featherstone, Mike Hepworth, and Byran Turner's anthology *The Body* (1991) consider diet, appetite, consumer culture, martial arts, aging, Nietzsche, and human emotions. These are topics worthy of an embodied reformulation.

A growing number of scholars have therefore attempted to reformulate the place—and significance—of the body in social thought. Much of this recent writing is outstanding. Two salient features of the new embodied discourse, however, weaken its overall scholarly impact. First, even the most insightful writers consider the body as a text that can be read and analyzed.[8] This analytical tack strips the body of its smells, tastes, textures and pains—its sensuousness. Second, recent writing on the body tends to be articulated in a curiously disembodied language. Consider, for example, Judith Butler's language in her well argued *Gender Trouble*:

The boundary of the body as well as the distinction between internal and external is established through the ejection and transvaluation of something originally part of identity into a defiling otherness. . . . What constitutes through the division of the "inner" and "outer" worlds of the subject is a border and boundary tenuously maintained for the purposes of social regulation and control. The boundary between inner and outer is confounded by those excremental passages in which the inner effectively becomes outer, and this excreting function becomes, as it were, the model by which other forms of identity-differentiation are accomplished. In effect, this is the model by which Others become shit. For inner and outer worlds to remain utterly distinct, the entire surface of the body would have to achieve an impossible imperme- ability. This sealing of its surfaces would constitute the seamless bound- ary of the subject; but this enclosure would invariably be exploded by precisely the excremental filth that it fears.[9]

The style of Butler's prose continuously evokes the texture of Foucault's language, which often employs sharply conceived spatial metaphors woven into a dense mosaic of abstract analy- sis. The persistence of such language in both feminist and post- structuralist writings on the body is ironic. In an abstract way the models and metaphors constructed by the likes of Foucault and Butler powerfully deconstruct the Cartesian edifice. But concomitantly their bloodless language reinforces the very prin- ciple they critique—the separation of mind and body, which, as we have seen, regulates and subjugates the very bodies they would liberate.

This argument may seem unreasonable. The analysis of com- plex philosophical and political issues usually requires intricate arguments expressed in a densely packed discourse. But such a requirement, I would argue, should not necessarily exclude sensuous expression. Put another way, discussions of the sensu- ous body require sensuous scholarship in which writers tack be- tween the analytical and the sensible, in which embodied form as well as disembodied logic constitute scholarly argument.

Sensuous Scholarship

Sensuous Scholarship is an attempt to reawaken profoundly the scholar's body by demonstrating how the fusion of the intelli- gible and the sensible can be applied to scholarly practices and representations. In anthropology, for example, it is especially important to incorporate into ethnographic works the sensuous body—its smells, tastes, textures, and sensations. Such inclusion is especially paramount in the ethnographic description of soci- eties in which the Eurocentric notion of text—and of textual interpretations—is not important. I have noted elsewhere why it is representationally and analytically important to consider how perception in non-Western societies devolves not simply from vision (and the linked metaphors of reading and writing) but also from smell, touch, taste, and hearing. In many societies these lower senses, all of which cry out for sensuous description, are central to the metaphoric organization of experience; they also trigger cultural memories.[10]

Critics may wonder why I should bother to write a book the purpose of which is to reawaken the scholar's body. Perhaps it would be better for the scholar's body to remain blissfully asleep in analytical nirvana? Maybe so. But why engage in the pursuit of knowledge, I wonder, if not to enrich the quality of life. For me, a fully sensuous scholarship is one path toward that felicitous end.

The book consists of six chapters grouped into three parts. The chapters in Part One, "Embodied Practices," demonstrate how sensuous nonvisual elements—taste and sound to be specific—constitute important aspects of the epistemology of Songhay-speaking peoples who today live in the Republics of Mali, Niger, and Benin in West Africa. Chapter 1, "The Sorcerer's Body," is an attempt to demonstrate how disembodied approaches to the anthropology of religion present only partial pictures of religious practices. Using material from fieldwork among Songhay sorcerers, I use sensuous description as well as logical exposition to argue that one learns about Songhay sorcery not through the assimilation of texts, but through the mastery of the body—through the vicissitudes of pain and illness. In Chapter 2, "The Griot's Tongue," I suggest that for Songhay griots, whose tongues articulate the past, history is not a subject or text to be mastered but a force that consumes the bodies of those who speak it.

Part Two, "Body and Memory," consists of chapters that suggest that memory (and history) is an embodied phenomenon. There are, of course, histories "from above" constituted by historical texts that are read re-read, interpreted, and reinterpreted. There are, as well, histories "from below" that are embodied in objects, song, movement, and the body. These are histories of the dispossessed. Chapter 3, "Embodying Colonial Memories," suggests that spirit possession constitutes an embodied history—from below—of the Songhay people. More specifically, it argues that the sensuousness of the Hauka spirits, which mimic West African colonial personages, triggers memories of colonial repression and power. Hauka spirit possession, I argue using a combination of sensuous and analytical language, has been used as a tool of empowerment. In Chapter 4, "'Conscious' Ain't Consciousness," the scene shifts from the "field" to the academy. It is a sensuous reading of several provocative texts that speak to the memory of the senses and the relation of body to memory.

Part Three, "Embodied Representations," attempts to demonstrate from a variety of perspectives how sensuous scholarship is transformed into text and image. Chapter 5, "Spaces, Places, and Fields," is an analysis of embodied power among Songhay peoples, but in New York City rather than the Republic of Niger. Here contemporary ethnography is attempted through a combination of sensuous description, historical exposition and theoretical argument. In it I suggest that the complex hybridity of transnational settings—Songhay street vendors in New York City—compels ethnographers to become sensuous scholars. In Chapter 6, "Artaud, Rouch, and the Cinema of Cruelty," I suggest that images on wooden stage and silver screen can be physiognomically transformative. Reacting to the power of the State to manipulate images and erase pain and suffering, I use the oeuvre of Antonin Artaud and Jean Rouch to suggest how scholars might construct "cruel" images that become cornerstones of a transformatively sensuous scholarship. In the Epilogue, "Sensuous Ways of Knowing," I attempt to delineate what a more sensuous scholarship might mean to scholars pondering the imponderables of the twenty-first century.

*   *   *

To accept sensuousness in scholarship is to eject the conceit of control in which mind and body, self and other are considered separate. It is indeed a humbling experience to recognize, like wise Songhay sorcerers and griots, that we do not consume sorcery, history, or knowledge; rather, it is history, sorcery, and knowledge that consume us. To accept sensuousness is, like the Songhay spirit medium or Sufi Saint, to lend one's body to the world and accept its complexities, tastes, structures, and smells.

By following Mojud's example, however, sensuous scholars need not give up their agency. Mojud didn't, nor did Antonin

Artaud or Jean Rouch. The sensuous scholar's agency, however, is a flexible one, in which the sensible and intelligible, denotative and evocative are linked. It is an agency imbued with what the late Italo Calvino called "lightness," the ability to make intellectual leaps to bridge gaps forged by the illusion of disparateness. It is also an agency in which scholars admit their errors of judgment and interpretation and struggle to improve their analytic and expository skills—all the better to cope with the burgeoning sociocultural complexities of globalization.

And so sensuous scholarship is ultimately a mixing of head and heart. It is an opening of one's being to the world—a welcoming. Such embodied hospitality is the secret of the great scholars, painters, poets, and filmmakers whose images and words resensualize us.

Why stay so long where your words are scattered
and doing no good? I've sent a letter a day
for a hundred days. Either you don't read the mail
or you've forgotten how to leave.

Let the letter read you. Come back.
No one understands who you are in that prison
for the stonefaced. You've escaped,
but still you sit there like a falcon
on the window ledge. You are both water and
steam, but you think you need something
to drink like a lion or deer.

How far is it? How far is the light of the moon
from the moon? How far is the taste of candy
from the lip? Every second you give away light.
We accept. We like this market.

Your love is a sweet poison we eat from your hand
to dissolve and drain away the ego-life
now spraying this fountain from us.
                                        —Rumi

PART 1
EMBODIED PRACTICES

Introduction: The Way of the Body

In his monumental *Philosophy and the Mirror of Nature* (1979) Richard Rorty painstakingly deconstructed the logical edifice of Western epistemology, leaving in its wake the dust of a thousand rarefied conversations. In later writings Rorty, among others, espoused a new pragmatism that emphasized local truths, community cohesion and civil conversation. Rorty and others did not claim that epistemology did not exist, but rather that epistemologies formulated and reformulated themselves in the interactional instabilities of local community life—all in a myriad of conversations that would edify the public.[1]

Rorty's work, of course, has considered the logical pitfalls of Western metaphysics, which, as we have already seen, is based in large measure on the Cartesian separation of mind and body, self and other. What of localized non-Western epistemologies? Can we consider them from a pragmatic framework? Should we?

The construction and deconstruction of Western metaphysics have been primarily disembodied visualist enterprises.[2] As I have noted elsewhere, vision is not always the singular sense that orders the experience of non-Western peoples. Among the Songhay peoples of Mali and Niger, whose religious and philosophical practices I discuss in Chapters 1 and 2, smell, taste, and sound contribute profoundly to the construction of their experience, which means that their epistemology is fundamentally embodied.[3] Songhay sorcerers and griots learn about power and history by "eating" it—ingesting odors and tastes, savoring textures and sounds.

As a complex, these chapters suggest why it is important for scholars to tune to local wavelengths of theory. These wavelengths, often constructed by way of the "lower" senses, by way of the body, have much to teach us about the ordering of experience, about the nature of epistemology in the contemporary world. Confronting the sensual constitution of local epistemologies is a first step toward a sensuous scholarship.

1
THE SORCERER'S BODY

In 1957 Claude Lévi-Strauss published his influential essay, "The Sorcerer and His Magic." Lévi-Strauss's essay built the foundation of a structuralist approach to the anthropological study of sorcery, healing, and religion. In a remarkable analysis Lévi-Strauss demonstrated that sorcerous ideologies were based on sociological fictions reinforced by magical sleight of hand. In the end the power of the sorcerer, he argued, rested not in an intrinsic power, but in the symbolic power of his or her relationship in the cultural continuum of illness and health.[1] Lévi-Strauss's argument is based on data gleaned not from his own fieldwork in Brazil but from the texts of other Americanists. The author of "The Sorcerer and His Magic" was therefore sensuously far removed from the material he analyzed with such persuasive objectivity. Distance from this and other materials helped him to produce a body of work in which structures are extracted from data.[2]

In 1937 E. E. Evans-Pritchard wrote the first and arguably one of the best studies of the religious beliefs of an African people. For Evans-Pritchard the ontological status of witchcraft or sorcery was less interesting than the non-Aristotelian logical system that supported a set of seemingly irrational beliefs. In his monumental *Witchcraft, Oracles, and Magic Among the Azande*, he compared and contrasted Zande and Western logic, suggesting that the "soul of witchcraft," a fireball that he once saw on a nocturnal stroll, was no more than a torch.[3] For Evans-Pritchard, then, Zande conceptions of witchcraft are considered not in and of themselves, but *as* a set of beliefs. Evans-Pritchard's pathbreaking work led to a spate of sociological studies of African witchcraft and sorcery which in the end were much less interesting than the master's cultural account of Zande belief.[4]

Although scholars have discerned vast theoretical differences between Lévi-Strauss and Evans-Pritchard, they share the same disembodied, objectivist epistemology. Lévi-Strauss's connection to objectivist epistemology is clear cut. The goal of his great body of work is to *uncover* hidden truths, structures, both formal and logical, which underlie the mind-boggling diversity of human practices in the world. Evans-Pritchard, too, embraces an objectivist epistemology. He used a disembodied theory of meaning and rationality to make sense of a foreign and ultimately bizarre system of belief. In both cases, however, disembodied principles are extracted from the field, from the other.

True to the heritage of the Enlightenment, Lévi-Strauss and Evans-Pritchard are scholars whose works extract explanatory truths from the contentious network of social relations which they attempt to observe. And yet, no matter the elegance of the disembodied analyses of Lévi-Strauss and Evans-Pritchard, they are bound to be incomplete, for they lead us far from the ideas, feelings, and sensibilities co-constituted with the people that these great authors sought to understand.

Attempting to avoid the representational and political pitfalls of disembodiment, a growing number of scholars, as indicated in the Prologue, have utilized the notion of the body—and embodiment—to criticize traditional predispositions in scholarly practices and writing. In much of this literature, as already noted, the body is idealized as a text. Considered as such, the body is "written" and "read." This is nowhere more apparent than in the postmodern *écriture féminine* movement in France, in which

Woman must write about her self: must write about women and bring women to writing, from which they have been driven away as violently as from their bodies—for the same reasons, by the same law, with the same fatal goal. Woman must put herself into the text—as into the world and into history—by her own movement.[5]

In Western society, women are struggling to put themselves into the text, into the world, and into history through their own movement. Accordingly, the notion of the body-as-text may be appropriate for the analysis of European culture in the era of late consumer capitalism. But is it not problematic to use the body as text metaphor in societies in which the body is felt and not read?[6] If so, we will need to develop a different tack for constructing an embodied alternative to the "mentalist" approaches to African religion.

In many North and West African societies learning is understood not in terms of "reading" and "writing," but in the gustatory terms of bodily consumption. This means that body and being are fused in consumptive or gustatory metaphors. Human beings eat and are eaten. People are transformed through their internal digestive processes.

The writer Paul Bowles, who has lived in North Africa for more than forty years, has well understood the existential importance of body metaphors in North Africa. In his perceptive and sensitive first novel, *The Sheltering Sky* (1976) he drafts a tale in terms of a classic quest in which two "lost" Americans attempt to find themselves in the Sahara. As the Americans venture farther and farther into the desert, they are consumed by it. Port Moresby's body is invaded by typhoid fever, which grows in his body until it saps it of its last breath. Life is transformed to death as typhoid, which symbolizes the invasion of the desert into Port's body, eats Port's being. In the end Port takes refuge beyond the sheltering sky. Bowles writes of pain, blood, excrement, and the desert wind to describe Port's final moments:

The pain could not go on. He opened his eyes, saw only the thin sky stretched across to protect him. Slowly the split would occur, the sky draw back, and he would see what he never had doubted lay behind advance upon him with the speed of a million winds. His cry was a separate thing beside him in the desert. It went on and on.[7]

His cry went on through the final image: the spots of raw bright blood on earth. Blood on excrement. The supreme moment high above the desert, when two elements, blood and excrement, long kept apart, merge. A black star appears, a point of darkness in the night's clarity. Point of darkness and gateway to repose. Reach out, pierce the fine fabric of the sheltering sky, take repose.[8]

At the death of her husband, Kit Moresby escapes into the desert and joins a Tuareg caravan. She is claimed by a Tuareg noble who takes her to his dwelling in a nameless Sahelian town. Her body is first consumed by her Tuareg captors, and then by exotic foods, by poison—by otherness. Just as the desert eats Port's body, it eats Kit's mind, driving her mad. To describe

Kit's state, Bowles again grounds his writing in the senses, in the body.

The sudden roar of the plane's motor behind her smashed the walls of the chamber where she lay. Before her eyes was the violent blue sky— nothing else. For an endless moment she looked into it. Like a great overpowering sound it destroyed everything in her mind, paralyzed her. Someone had once said to her that the sky hides the horror that lies above. Unblinking, she fixed the solid emptiness, and the anguish began to move in her. At any moment the rip can occur, the edges fly back, and the giant maw will be revealed.[9]

Through gustatory metaphors, the Songhay people of Mali and Niger also fuse body and being. The stomach is considered the site of human personality and agency. Social relations are considered in terms of eating. Consider the following Songhay expressions.

Ay ga borodin nga
I am going to eat that particular person
Ay ga habu nga
I am going to eat the market

In the first expression, knowledge of the other person is eaten. Individuals will get to know the other so well that they will ingest the other's being. In Songhay, people consume otherness, but are also consumed by otherness. In the second expression, individuals eat the market if they master it. If they return home without profit, the market will have eaten them.

In Songhay, gustatory metaphors are also used to understand history and the power of sorcerers. Griots (bards), who are the custodians of the oral tradition, say:

Ay ga don bori sonni nga
I eat the words of the ancestors

As in the other statements, this one also implies that the words of ancestors also eat the griots—consume them, and by extension—transform their being (see Chapter 2). The sorcerers of Songhay, called *sohanci*, literally eat their power and are eaten by it. They say:

Boro ga nga kusu, ama kusu mo no ga boro nga.
A person eats kusu (food of power), but the food of power
also eats a person.

In other words, when sorcerers eat the *kusu* of initiation, they
become full, which means they enter a network of sorcerous relations in which they eat or are eaten, for if sorcerers' bodies are
emptied, they become ill, go insane, or die, their bodies consumed much as the desert consumed the body of Port Moresby
and the mind of Kit Moresby.

In the remainder of this chapter, I will attempt to demonstrate further the cultural importance of the sentient body in
Songhay by presenting a long, sensuously explicit narrative that
describes how Songhay sorcerery consumed my body. I employ
this narrative to demonstrate what Songhay sorcerers have long
known: that one learns about (Songhay) sorcery through the
body. I also employ it to suggest how in a sensuous scholarship
narrative can be used felicitiously to construct a scholary argument. An approach as in Africa by western scholars that privi-
leges the mind over body or which considers body as text will
not do.

Fractured Fieldwork

My research trip to the Republic of Niger in March 1990 was
an unmitigated disaster. I went there to gather data I needed
to write a biography of a family of Songhay sorcerer-warriors. I
scheduled interviews well in advance; advance planning would
guarantee, or so I thought, that *X* would be in village *Y* when
I arrived. During the projected two and a half months of fieldwork, I was to travel in the bush, record numerous life histories,
and lecture at the University of Niamey. There would even be
time to attend several spirit possession ceremonies and sacri-
fices that would take place in early May, just before my departure.

I abruptly terminated my field journey, leaving after only
three weeks in Niger.

My first week in Niamey and Tillaberi was without incident. I
saw old friends, recorded a life history, observed a sacrifice, and
made arrangements to lecture at the research center.

At the beginning of the second week, in Tillaberi, the village in which I had periodically resided since 1970, the older son of my late teacher Adamu Jenitongo prepared for me some six-powder *kusu* (magic cake). Sensing that I needed "fortification" for the upcoming year, he poured his powders onto a piece of white cloth, creating a small yellow dune streaked with ribbons of black, red, and green. Using his thumb and middle finger, he distributed the powder into a small clay pot, which he had filled with water. After he had recited appropriate incantations, he lit a small fire, placed the clay pot above it, and fanned the flames until the mixture boiled. Gradually he added millet flour and stirred the concoction until it thickened into a brownish-green paste. Once this "food without sauce," as *kusu* is called, had cooled, we ate it.

My problems began the next day when I returned to Niamey: heavy legs and back pain, the symptoms of *weyna,* what the Songhay term a "hot" illness. I went to a herbalist, who gave me a powdered mixture of two roots which I was to prepare as a decoction. I drank three doses of the decoction and felt measurably better.

Two days later, still in Niamey, I was the front seat passenger in a Renault that rear-ended a Mercedes whose driver had stopped suddenly in front of us to talk with a pedestrian. The impact accordion-pleated the front of the Renault and threw me against the padded sun visor, bruising my forehead. A passenger in the back seat bruised her knees: no serious injuries, just rattled nerves.

The bruise on my forehead had turned a deep blue by the time I went to a wedding ceremony: cool night air, thumping don-don drums, relentless praise-singing, all part of the bard's extortion of ritual gifts from Songhay nobles. It is the license of this group of "captives" to behave aggressively. And they do! Usually I am happy to participate in these ceremonies, but on that night I felt tired and headachy. I recognized the onset of malaria. No big deal, I told myself. I'll simply give myself the "cure," as I had done on many occasions in years past. I dosed myself with chloroquine phosphate and went to bed, only to awake in the middle of the night in a pool of sweat. My head throbbed. In the morning I took a few more chloroquine tablets, but my condition didn't change. By the next day my eyes

Figure 1. Adamu Jenitongo, Songhay sorcerer extraordinaire.

blazed with fever. I took two more chloroquine tablets. By noon, my aching body was incandescent with fever. A visiting physician told me that I had contracted a chloroquine-resistant malaria. She gave me three tablets of a different, stronger drug.

"That will break your fever," she said.

"That" also "broke" my body. I remained in bed, my legs as heavy as water-soaked logs.

Days passed. Periodically, I felt strong enough to see people. Unsteadily, I would dress and leave my house. Three days into my third week in Niger, I got a ride to the research center. When I tried to walk up the stairs to the office of a Senegalese colleague, I couldn't make it beyond the fourth step. My colleague called his chauffeur, who returned me to my dwelling. Given these circumstances, in which so much had happened so quickly, I decided to leave Niger at once. The next day I arranged a flight to Paris and left Niger two days later, exactly three weeks after I had arrived.

Had I returned home too hastily? Had I given up too soon? Had I succumbed to failure too easily? Probably. As is often said among anthropologists, however, "When in doubt, leave!" My Songhay friends presented me with a more troubling interpretation. They said invariably:

Wati kan boro fonda hasara, boro ma ye hu
When one's path has been spoiled, he or she should return home

Soumana Yacouba, a Niamey herbalist and healer, told me to go home.

"Your path has been spoiled," he said. "You didn't pay attention this year. There are people here who wish you ill, but you didn't come to see me *before* you started your work. Your baba [Adamu Jenitongo] can no longer protect you from others. Next time, you'll come to my house before you begin your work. Go home and strengthen yourself."

I explained what had happened to a Nigerien social scientist.

"Go home," he said. "Go home and gather your strength."

I explained what had happened to an official in Niger's Ministry of Foreign Affairs.

"Go home," he said. "Your path has been blocked, spoiled.

You must go home and recuperate."

"Yes," I said. "I think you're right."

"Your baba is no longer here," he said, "and in the world that you walk, people are always testing one another. Sorcerers are the offspring of fire; they can't contain their power. Go home and be more judicious when you return. May God shame the person who sent this to you."

And so I returned home, having learned through my body a lesson in Songhay sorcery.

The Etiology of *Sambeli*

In and of itself, this litany of events is unremarkable. Many if not most fieldworkers in Africa have suffered from malarial attacks; some have been involved in automobile accidents. What is interesting here is the nature of the ethnographer's implication in things Songhay. Most of my Nigerien friends, scholars and farmers alike, believed that I had been the victim of a sorcerous attack, *sambeli*, for even if individuals have taken only a few steps on sorcery's path as I had done years earlier, their bodies, they told me, become targets. Once sorcerers have eaten power, their bodies can be consumed by power.

In the practice of Songhay sorcery, *sambeli* is the act of sending fear and/or sickness to a victim. Fear can be sent by reciting the victim's name followed by a series of incantations as one winds copper wire around certain objects. This rite is performed over a sorcerer's altar. Once fear has been "sent," the recipient, who may have insulted the sorcerer or the sorcerer's work, may well be frightened as her or his being is consumed by the sorcerer's power. In this way victims *understand.* They are humbled into a profound respect of the sorcerer's science, if not the sorcerers themselves.

Sickness is sent in an altogether different manner. A small number of sorcerers possess a special bow and arrow which is associated with a particular spirit in the Songhay pantheon. On rare occasions, the sorcerers take the bow and speak to the arrow—from their hearts. They then recite the name of their victim, usually a rival, and shoot the arrow, which carries sickness to its target. If the sorcerer's aim is good, victims feel a sharp pain in one of their legs as if someone is pricking them with a knife. If victims are unprotected by magic rings or other amulets, the sickness will spread, resulting in partial paralysis and sometimes death. People who are well protected evade the arrow's path.

When Adamu Jenitongo took me into his confidence and made me a recipient of his secret knowledge in 1977, he thrust me into the Songhay world of sorcery, which I have elsewhere described in vivid detail.[10] Briefly, it is an amoral world, in which social rights and obligations are meaningless. The void created by this amorality is filled with power—of rival sorcerers, themselves offspring of fire, so brimming with force that they have little control over their spiteful tastes and desires.[11] One step into the world of Songhay sorcery means that one joins forever more an ever-changing network of sorcerers, some of whom are allies who may become enemies, some of whom are enemies who may become allies, all of whom are rivals for power. In this world of spite and jealousy, the sentient body is the arena of power, for one literally eats power and is eaten by it.

Sohanci have long used the body to learn. They ingest *guru kusu*, which protects them from knives and other sharp objects. If the *kusu* has been prepared correctly, a sharp knife will not cut through the sorcerer's skin. A master sohanci revealing his or her secret to apprentices teaches them the requisite incantations and how to identify the plants and animal parts that comprise the recipe. Then the master tells the students to prepare the *kusu*. When the students have eaten and digested the paste they have prepared, the master takes a sharp knife and attempts to slice it deeply into their arms. If the knife "refuses to cut," the student has mastered the lesson. If blood spurts from a fresh wound, the student has failed and will have to prepare a another batch of *kusu*.[12] Students continue to prepare *kusu* until they either "get it right" or give up their apprenticeships. Many sohanci have knife scars on their arms. For them, the body is the locus of learning; scars signal the toughness of their paths to mastery.

The Etiology of Apprenticeship

So far, I have described the etiology of *sambeli*. But to comprehend why my Nigerien friends thought that sickness had been

sent to me, I must briefly present the history of my appretice-
ship to Adamu Jenitongo. This history demonstrates graphically
how Songhay sorcery is learned through the body; it also underscores the applicability of the sensuous perspective I am advo-
cating in this book.

From the beginning of my apprenticeship in Songhay sorcery
I began to eat power in the form of magic cake or *kusu*. *Kusu*
consists of millet flour in which are cooked pulverized plants,
which have been imbued with powerful ancestral words. When
I ate my first batch of *kusu* in 1977, my initiator Koda Mounmouni told me that "power" had attached itself to my intestines.
Witches, he said, could no longer look me in the eye. Unprotected men and women, he told me, would fear me. Although
fellow sorcerers tested my strength, I emerged from this intial
period of initiation unscathed and confident—cocky and fool-
ish enough to practice what I had learned. That year I was
asked to do "work" by an acquaintance who had confidence in
the progress of my apprenticeship. Not believing that a simple
ritual act might have sentient consequences, I performed the
appropriate rite.

In 1979 I learned that my "work," the recitation of an incantation over the organ of a certain kind of chicken, which
was then buried under the threshold of the target's house, had
physical results. The body of the target had not been affected,
but his sister's face had become paralyzed, a paralysis which
relaxed when she returned to France.[13] I became temporarily
paralyzed, during that same trip in 1979, in Wanzerbe, the village of unrivaled Songhay power. Although the event terrified
me, it pleased my teachers. They said that my paralysis had pro-
pelled me into the world of Songhay sorcery. Indeed, for the
first time I understood the Songhay maxim:

> sohancitarey manti horey no
> The sohanci's work is no game

For Songhay practitioners, sorcery is not merely a set of beliefs, as Evans-Pritchard would have it; rather, it carries with
it real consequences—bodily consequences. In Songhay, sorcerers "eat" and are "eaten." "Are you full (of food)?" "How
much do you know?" These questions are answered when a rival

tests a fellow sorcerer through attack. If sorcerers resist attacks through whatever means, they are stronger and their attackers become respectful. If sorcerers become sick, their rivals have bettered them: they have won and demonstrated their superior knowledge and power. The marks of these battles are not only inscribed in sorcerers' consciousness, they are worn in and on their (extended) bodies. They walk with a limp. Their arms are impaired. They are blind. Their children die young. Their betrothed die just before their marriages are consummated. In the Songhay world, sorcerous embodiment always exacts a high price.

As a result of my paralysis, a Wanzerbé sorcerer invited me into her house to learn her secrets. At the time a dangerous hubris excluded a more salutary reasonableness. I had fought the Wanzerbe sorcerer and had won. Alas, my victory was an empty one, for it attracted new enemies, people who wanted to use me—and my body—to better themselves. Through my body I had discovered a terrifying world.

In subsequent years Adamu Jenitongo gave me rings, bracelets, and belts that had "drunk" the powerful blood of sacrificial animals. These power objects, like the sorcerer's body, must be fed with food and drink. He told me to wear these rings on the third finger of my left hand, the bracelets on my left wrist, the belts around my waist. He said that this "medicine" would work if and only if it "touched" my body, completing, as it were, the embodied recipe of power. I accepted these objects and wore them.

In 1984 Adamu Jenitongo not only revealed to me his extensive knowledge of plants, but gave me two of his most precious and powerful objects: a large copper ring and a small white stone as smooth as an egg shell. He said that the ring, which I was to keep in my left pocket or wear around my neck, would maintain contact between him and me even after his death. He said that the stone, which, like the ring, had been his father's power object, would keep me straight on my path and well anchored to the world of practical affairs.

Wisely, I hid the stone immediately. Foolishly, I attached the large copper ring to a black cord and put it around my neck. During the considerable heat of the next afternoon, I walked around the compound shirtless, unthinkingly revealing my prize to family members and visitors alike. The sohanci's older son saw the ring and frowned. The sohanci's younger son saw the ring and grimaced. They resented the fact that I had learned more from their biological father than they had.

"They're not ready yet," Adamu Jenitongo would always say. "They're not ready yet."

Maybe so, but *they* thought they were.

Other people in the family came to envy my good fortune. Adamu Jenitongo's older brother's youngest son coveted his "father"'s secrets, his power. He spent many afternoons in the compound, conversing and helping to organize spirit possession ceremonies. He hoped that one day the old man would say: "Come into my hut," a gloss for, "I have something to teach you, my son." But Adamu Jenitongo did not trust his nephew's character, and so he refused to share his considerable knowledge with him. Impotent against his powerful uncle, the nephew took out his frustrations on me, a seemingly vulnerable white man.

The sohanci's second wife saw me as a threat. My presence could and would divert power away from her son. A sharp-tongued woman, she frequently told me that the sohanci's elder son and potential heir had a black heart. Unlike her son, whose heart was as white as a dove's, the older son was not to be trusted with money or powerful knowledge. When it became clear that the sohanci had chosen the older son to receive his most precious secrets, she could contain herself no longer. In Songhay it is said that *bab'izey*, sons of one father but of different mothers, are a source of all great jealousy and discord. Nothing could be more accurate in the case of Adamu Jenitongo's compound.

While Adamu Jenitongo was alive, the lid still covered the family's pot of trouble. With Adamu Jenitongo's death in March 1988, jealousy and rivalry fanned the fires of the family's discontent, blowing the lid off the pot.

Adamu Jenitongo's death brought me to Tillaberi, Niger to sit with the mourning family. Sometimes funerals are occasions during which long-lost relatives materialize. Such was the case in Tillaberi in March 1988. I met several of Adamu Jenitongo's relatives from Simiri-Sohanci. One classificatory "son," some twenty years my senior, had heard that I had learned many secrets from his "father." He coveted the "medicine" I wore on my left hand. He had heard that I was full—of powerful *kusu*. He wanted some for himself.

"Did you bring your shells?" he asked me.

"Shells?"

"You know, the cowrie shells that see the past as well as the future."

Fearing just such a question, I had left the shells in the United States. "No, I didn't," I responded.

"Why didn't you bring them? Some of us want to learn to read them. We in Simiri didn't get anything from Baba. We want you to teach us."

"But I don't know enough to teach you, and I didn't bring the shells."

This man from Simiri left Tillaberi disappointed, but no more so than Adamu Jenitongo's sister, who had declared days before my arrival that after her brother's death I would never return to Tillaberi. When Adamu Jenitongo died, she confronted Adamu Jenitongo's elder son. She wanted him to give her all Adamu Jenitongo's ritual and power objects: the rings he wore on his fingers; the bracelets he wore on his wrists; the stones he kept with his clairvoyant shells; the special belts he wore around his waist; the spirit possession objects and costumes he hid in the dark recesses of his spirit hut. The object she coveted the most, however, was the *lolo*, the sohanci's iron staff, encrusted by hundreds of years of sacrificial blood.

The older son politely denied her demands. Before his death Adamu Jenitongo had made his sons promise to keep all his *goy gine* or work things. "Don't give them to anyone. They will come and demand my things, but they are for the [immediate] family, no one else."

In the past, a sohanci's work things were given to his oldest surviving brother. In the past the solidarity of Songhay patrilineages usually ensured the brotherly inheritance of power objects. The Jenitongo lineage, however, has had a long history of fragmentation. In Adamu Jenitongo's case the two candidates for his "things" lived in Simiri-Sohanci. One brother didn't visit the family after Adamu Jenitongo's death. The other, who spent several days with the mourners in Tillaberi, had seen Adamu Jenitongo only a few times during the previous twenty years. As

Adamu Jenitongo told his older son before he died: "They did nothing for me when I was alive. I'll do nothing for them when I'm dead."

And so Adamu Jenitongo's objects of power remained in his Tillaberi compound under the guardianship of his older son, who gave his younger brother most of his father's spirit possession objects. Neither son had the age or rank to wear most of Adamu Jenitongo's rings. Before he died, however, Adamu Jenitongo told the older son that after his death he should place three of his copper rings on a mat in the company of his brother and myself. During my 1988 visit the older son followed his father's instructions. We each selected our rings and put them on the third finger of our left hands—the finger of power.

In March 1988 people noticed the rings, which spurred jealousy among people in Tillaberi as well as among Adamu Jenitongo's kin in Simiri-Sohanci. Even before my departure in April, rumors were circulating widely in Tillaberi. "They" had received Adamu Jenitongo's greatest secrets. Even though "they" have received power, "they" are young and ignorant. Accordingly, a number of townspeople attempted to secure these objects.

The younger son also felt shortchanged. Had his older brother received more power than he? The forty-day mourning period was no time to resolve these putative inequities. But townspeople did have the younger brother's ear. They tried to curry favor with him as a way of gaining access to Adamu Jenitongo's powerful and potentially profitable treasures. More spite, more seething resentment, more fuel for the fire burning through the compound.

In December 1988 I returned to Tillaberi to help organize Adamu Jenitongo's *kuma*, a spirit possession ceremony that marks the end of the period of mourning following a spirit possession priest's death. The *kuma* is usually celebrated 40 days following the priest's death. In Adamu Jenitongo's case, the older son postponed the ceremony until I could attend.

Following his father's instructions, the older son sacrificed one red and one white chicken over a gourd filled with whittled pieces of a certain tree root. These we buried at the threshold of the compound and in front of all the doors of the dwellings.

We also buried these sticks at the compound's center and at each of its corners. Three days before the ceremony, the older son prepared *kusu* for everyone to protect us from "enemies." Two days before the ceremony he sacrificed a black chicken. This blood, the older son said, would create a barrier between "us" and "them."

One day before the ceremony we heard that Adamu Jenitongo's nephew had slunk out to the bush in the middle of the night. Aided by an accomplice, he held a black chicken above his head and killed it by twisting its neck. He threw the carcass in the direction of Adamu Jenitongo's compound: death magic.

A war was on, but the older son's protection repelled the nephew's advance. The evening before the ceremony, a neighbor guarded the compound, thinking that someone, namely, Adamu Jenitongo's nephew, would attempt to spoil the *kuma*. The night passed without incident.

At noon the next day we filed out into the bush, the space of the spirits. At a crossroads in the bush, a neighboring so-hanci recited several incantations over a clay pot filled with water in which he mixed pulverized tree barks and perfumes. People wept loudly, remembering with sadness the passing of a great man. The neighboring sohanci called us to present ourselves to the pot of purification. He gave the younger son and me a small container of the ablution. We walked into the bush, stripped, and washed from our bodies the filth of Adamu Jenitongo's death.

In Songhay, the filth of death enters the mourner's body, making her or him sluggish, indecisive, and muddle-headed, a truly embodied state. If death is not cleansed from the body, it, like power, will consume individuals, making them chronically sick, driving them mad, or killing them.

We cleansed ourselves of the filth of Adamu Jenitongo's death; filth emerged from our pores. The younger son took a deep breath. I smiled.

We walked back to the compound, where the musicians played the airs and rhythms of Adamu Jenitongo's spirits. Would one of his departed spirits choose a new medium that day? As it turned out, only one of Adamu Jenitongo's four spirits selected a new medium, Daouda Godji, the chief violinist of the Tillaberi

Figure 2. Koda Mounmouni, the embodiment of sorcery in Mehanna, Niger.

spirit possession troupe. By late afternoon, the last of the spirit mediums had left the compound. Adamu Jenitongo's *kuma* was now an indelible memory.

By the time I returned to Niger in March 1990, Adamu Jenitongo's compound was seething with resentment and jealousy. The two brothers argued incessantly. The older son argued with the younger son's mother. The younger son's mother argued with anyone, anywhere. Prior to my arrival in 1990, tragedy struck. After years of preparation and financial sacrifice, the older son had arranged to marry the daughter of the sohanci of the next village, Tillakayna. One week before his fifteen-year-old bride was to come to live with her new husband, she fell seriously ill and died. Somehow, the older son arranged another marriage at considerable expense.

To make matters even worse, people in the Tillaberi spirit possession troupe had been hatching plots to acquire Adamu Jenitongo's "work things." Following his death in 1988, these people attempted to corner the Tillaberi spirit possession market: expensive cures for spirit illnesses; fees for holding ceremonies in their compounds; fees for their services as priests and priestesses; fees for "work" (sorcery). For them, the older son was a roadblock on the path to economic prosperity, for they assumed, rightly, that he had received wisdom and power objects from his father. But they did not know whether he had yet "arrived." It takes years for power to materialize, for one's path to open, as the Songhay say. And so according to him, rivals in Tillaberi wanted to test his abilities by sending sickness (*sambeli*)—to me. In 1990 they celebrated their success. Such is the older son's theory of what happened to me during my last trip to Niger.

Although he was uncertain of the source of the *sambeli*, he was certain that my body had been pierced by the arrow of "sickness." My body, in Songhay terms, had been partially consumed by power. Other people in Niger, scholars as well as herbalists, agreed.

When one's path has been spoiled, one must return home.

As in the past, the body had been an arena of learning about Songhay sorcery. Once individuals have eaten the *kusu* of initiation, they are *implicated* in a system of sorcerous relations, a network of rivalry in which the body eats power and power eats the body.

Embodied Sorcery, Sensuous Reason

Like most scholars, anthropologists usually confront social reality through a disembodied gaze. Like most scholars, anthropologists usually believe that the tangled skein of human relations can be unknotted and explained. In the arena of sorcery this conceit means that one can probe behind a veil of troublesome confusions and discover principles, patterns, and hypotheses. Such epistemolgoical confidence was once the hallmark of the natural sciences and continues to be the hallmark of objectivist social science.

In this chapter I have employed a long personal narrative to advocate an embodied approach to the anthropology of religion. Throughout my apprenticeship the body—my body—was the locus of sorcerous learning. These learning experiences compelled me to place a premium on the contingent nature of "experience-in-the-field."

Michael Jackson writes about some of these issues in his 1989 book, *Paths to a Clearing: Radical Empiricism and Ethnographic Inquiry.*

The importance of this view for anthropology is that it stresses the ethnographer's *interactions* with those he or she lives with and studies, while urging us to clarify ways in which our knowledge is grounded in our practical, personal, and participatory experience in the field as much as our detached observations. Unlike traditional empiricism, which draws a definite boundary between observer and observed, between method and object, radical empiricism denies the validity of such cuts and makes the *interplay* between these domains the focus of its interest.[14]

Here Jackson focuses on the contingent and highly complex relationship between the observer and the observed. He writes that

anthropology involves *reciprocal* activities and *inter*experience [Devereux 1967: 18–31]. This makes the relationship between knower and known infinitely more complicated. Indeed, given the arduous conditions of fieldwork, the ambiguity of conversations in a foreign tongue, differences of temperament, age, and gender between ourselves and our informants, and the changing theoretical models we are heir to, it is likely that "objectivity" serves more as a magical token, bolstering our sense of self in disorienting situations, than as a scientific method for describing those situations as they really are. The orderly systems and determinate structures we describe are not mirror images of social reality so much as defenses we build against the unsystematic, unstructured nature of our *experiences* within that reality.[15]

To put the matter bluntly, we often avoid acknowledging the contingent nature of situated experience, which distances us from the ambiguous, from the tangential, from the external textures and sensuous processes of our bodies. Comprehension of Songhay sorcery demands "the presence, not the absence, of the ethnographer."[16]

The full presence of the ethnographer's body in the field also demands a fuller sensual awareness of the smells, tastes, sounds and textures of life among the others. It demands, as I have stated in the Prologue, that ethnographers open themselves to others and absorb their worlds. Such is the meaning of embodiment. For ethnographers embodiment is more than the realization that our bodily experience gives metaphorical meaning to our experience; it is rather the realization that, like Songhay sorcerers, we too are consumed by the sensual world, that ethnographic things capture us through our bodies, that profound lessons are learned when sharp pains streak up our legs in the middle of the night.

2
THE GRIOT'S TONGUE

Me ra hari si denji wi
"One mouthful of water will not douse a fire"

Boro ma bon bey za borey man'inga bey
"People must know themselves before they let others know
them"

—Songhay proverbs

During my long apprenticeship to Adamu Jenitongo, almost all
of our discussions took place under a lonely acacia in the center of his compound. One afternoon toward the end of his life,
the old man asked me into his spirit hut. My heart leaped with
expectation, for I knew that such an invitation—rarely if ever
given—meant that the time had come for the master to impart
important knowledge to me.

"You have learned much over the years," he insisted.

I said nothing.

"You have learned our words and about our plants."

"I have tried to listen," I responded.

"You have learned much, my son, but you know little."

Again, I said nothing.

"It is easy to learn our incantations, and even a child can
learn to identify plants. And with God's blessing one day soon
you'll be ready to learn something important."

"What, Baba, surpasses the knowledge of plants and sorcery?"

"Awareness of plants and sorcery," he said, "means little without a knowledge of history. Power, my son, comes from history."

*   *   *

Among the peoples who live in the West African Sahel there are many proverbs that speak to the notion of preparation. Like the Songhay sorcerers we considered in the previous chapter, the bodies of griots or bards must be thoroughly prepared—to talk social life. Griots must apprentice themselves to masters for as long as thirty years before they are deemed ready to recite their poetry. There are two stages in the training of griots among the Songhay-speaking peoples of the Republics of Mali and Niger. First, griots must master a body of rudimentary knowledge—in their case, the words of Songhay history. Such mastery, however, is insufficient, for griots must also master themselves to embody the power of history. This means that they must learn to dispossess their "selves" from the "old words" they have learned. The words that constitute history are much too powerful to be "owned" by any one person or group of people; rather these words "own" those who speak them. Accomplished griots do not "own" history; rather, they are possessed by the forces of the past. By decentering themselves from history and the forces of social life, these griots are infused with great dignity. In time their tongues become ripe for history. Only these griots are capable of meeting the greatest challenge: imparting social knowledge to the next generation.

For several Songhay elders, ethnographers are griots. Ethnographers, like griots, must learn history and cultural knowledge. Griots are strictly oral practitioners; ethnographers recount what they have "mastered" in printed words or in filmed images. There is a longstanding tradition of scribes in Songhay which dates to the fifteenth century and the court of Askia Mohammed Touré.[1] Songhay populations have sensed the griotic possibilities of film since the early 1920s. Many Songhay elders think the films of Jean Rouch (films on Songhay possession, magic, and migration) are the tales of a griot, albeit a cinematic one. When ethnographers are asked to read their works to gatherings of Songhay elders, they, too, are considered griots.

Ethnographers, however, usually consider themselves scholars, not griots. They prepare themselves for their life's work in a manner altogether different from that of the griot. They read canonic texts, debate arcane theories, take examinations, conduct research, and "writeup" or "edit" the results of their data-gatherings. Sometimes they engage in follow-up research. This preparation and "work" results in a body of scholarly essays, monographs, and films. In most cases social scientists attempt to tease from the tangled threads of social life insights that will make a contribution to social theory.

For most Songhay elders, the theoretical results of social science research are meaningless. They don't care whether monographs on the Songhay refine theories of cultural hermeneutics or clear up the murkiness of the postmodern condition. They *do* care about how well their tale is told. They care about the poetic quality of their story. They especially care about whether scholars demonstrate a healthy respect for the "old words." They care about whether scholars are humbled by history, which consumes the bodies of those who attempt to talk it, write it, or film it. They care about the nature of the responsibility that scholars take for their words and images. For most Songhay elders the ultimate test of scholars is whether their words and images enable the young to uncover their past and discover their future.

In the remainder of this chapter I suggest that when social scientists attempt to depict social life—to write or film lives—they should incorporate the griot's historically conscientious and respectfully decentered conception and practice of depicting social life, a profoundly embodied conception and practice of ethnography that reverberates with the tension between the political and the poetic. Such an incorporation requires that scholars spend long periods of time apprenticing themselves to elders, long periods of time mastering knowledge. This also impels scholars to complement their explorations in social theory with tales of a people that are respectful and poetically evocative. Following this senuous path, scholars may well understand how a mouthful of water can't douse a fire, and why griots must know themselves before they let others know them. Such is a central attribute in a sensuous scholarship.

The Griot in Sahelian West Africa

In Sahelian West Africa griots are considered masters of words. From a Sahelian perspective, however, this means that griots have been mastered by words, that words have eaten them. African scholars like Ahmadou Hampaté Ba consider griots the "archivists" of their cultures. They are "great depositaries, who, it can be said, are the living memory of Africa."[2] The words that have mastered the griot are said to embody great power. Among the Mande-speaking peoples in and around the Republic of Mali, words are dangerous for they are infused with *nyama*, which Charles Bird translates as "energy of action."[3] Among the Mande, only the *nyamakala*, a "casted" branch of Mande society, consisting of musicians, leather workers, smiths, and griots, can manipulate the potentially dangerous force of *nyama*.[4] In Sahelian West Africa "griots are spokespersons and ambassadors, matrimonial go-betweens, genealogists and historians, advisors and court-jesters."[5] In some griotic performances, especially the recitation of genealogies, there is intense negotiation between a patron and her or his griot. Sometimes the griot will stop the recitation of a genealogy to negotiate or, more likely, renegotiate a fee. All of this is tied to the mutual recognition of status. In the recitation of epic poetry, these kinds of negotiations take place before the performance. No matter when the negotiations take place, griots are very much aware of their audiences and will sometimes footnote their performances. Judith Irvine's work on Wolof griots articulates the complexities of this negotiation and how it is tied to the historical dimensions of the griot's performance.[6]

As a medium, film has more affinity to the griot's performance than do ethnographies articulated in prose. Film can recreate the fluidity of cultural performance in ways that prose cannot. When Jean Rouch first screened his films in Ayoru, (Niger), and along the Bandiagara Cliffs in Dogon Country (Mali), people remarked: "You are a true griot. Your films have enabled the dead to live again." Several Songhay elders also consider my ethnographies griotic tales. Adamu Jenitongo once said to me: "You are my griot. I give you my words and you write them. If my words live forever, I shall live forever." He believed that one day his grandchildren would read about him in my writings. He also thought it was important for me to be his griot to Americans. To his dying days he wanted American readers to know some of the feats of the Songhay past; he wanted readers to know something of the sohanci's courage and daring.

The subject of the griot in West Africa is a vast one. The concern here, however, is principally with the griot as go-between, as an embodied articulator of history, as the teller of tales of

Figure 3. Ayouba Tessa Chants a Version of the Epic of Askia
Mohammed at Garbey Kuru, Niger, April 11, 1981. Photo: Thomas A.
Hale.

both social and political significance. John Chernoff's longterm
research among the Dagbamba of northern Ghana suggests that
drummers are the griots of that society. Dagbon drummers are
"owned" by the "old words." They learn and teach the history of
Dagbon. They are masters of kinship, religion, culture, and philosophy. Chernoff describes the work of his teacher, Ibrahim:

He has many names. His name is Ibrahim. His name is "Father Drummer." His name is "What a human being refuses, God will take and
make well." His name is "Wisdom has no end." How a person comes to
have such names is another story among the stories in this book, but

he is one man among many like him. He speaks the words of those he knows and has known and the words of those who gave birth to him and have passed away. He represents them, and he is old because he holds their words. He and his colleagues are all masters of words, but they do not write. Their knowledge is sustained by memory; it is communicated in public places by sound and movement, by singing, by drumming, by dancing.[7]

Even if griots demonstrate a certain pride of performance, the most accomplished ones never forget their humble embodied relation to the power of words and the forces of history. In West Africa, then, the greatest griots are "owned" by the oral tradition which means that they are possessed by "total knowledge."[8]

What conditions construct and shape this "total knowledge"? What factors influence the transmission of this "total knowledge"? How does the griot's tongue articulate history and social life? Are there affinities between the quandaries of talking social life and those posed by writing or filming social life? Are there affinities between griots and ethnographers, who, usually have the difficult task of *representing* someone else's social life?

Griots and the Death of the Author

During the past twenty years, North American scholars in the humanities and social sciences have been greatly influenced by poststructualist criticism. This maze of ideas, or so we are led to believe, has eroded the last vestiges of objective representation, determinacy, and (social) science. In a perilously fragmented world in which space and time are likewise exploded, the death of God, proclaimed by Nietzsche and Dostoyevsky, has led ultimately to the death of "man," and to the death of the author.[9]

The foundation of Roland Barthes's admittedly ironic view of authorship is that one does not write in isolation from cultural and historical conditions. Writing is therefore not context-free; it is shaped by political and sociological factors. To borrow Derrida's now famous phrase, writing is always already there. Situated in the vortex of ever-changing political, social, historical, and cultural realities, writers choose among various voices, themselves contingent on social and historical factors. In this way author-ity is rendered problematic. Can authors speak for themselves? Can they speak for others? Or do their often conflicting voices constitute a patchwork of the contingent conditions of sociality? In the contemporary world as it is perceived by many poststructuralist and postmodernist critics, the self, hence the author, is opaque. As a consequence "dead" authors live on as dispossessed writers who speak in what Barthes called "the middle voice":

[The] middle voice corresponds exactly to the state of the verb to write: today to write is to make one's self the center of the action of speech [parole]; it is to effect writing in being affected oneself; it is to leave the writer [scripteur] inside the writing, not as a psychological subject . . . but as agent of action.[10]

In the middle voice there is no authorial agency. Words are articulated, but no agent is associated with the signified action. An apt example is the French intransitive verb, *se manger*. The expression *ça se mange* (this eats itself) constitutes an indirect, agentless commentary on the (good) quality of food. Sociolinguistically, the use of such an expression decenters the subject in a manner similar to the way griots decenter themselves during a performance. With the subject decentered, writing or performing becomes the site of an "authorless" text. From a contemporary perspective, the arrogance of "living authors" who constructed their subjectivity through the objectification of others has created much shame that has survived their deaths.[11] Such a tack would be unthinkable to the seasoned griot. Put another way, dead authors become writers who no longer "own" language; they are, like the griot, embodied—"owned"—by language.

During the 1980s, Barthes's death-of-the-author syndrome affected the social sciences in a major way. Anthropologists, for example, began to reflect on their own ethnographic practices. Such reflections, first hinted at by Clifford Geertz in the 1970s, produced a new discourse that bifurcated into two paths. Followers of the first path traveled in the direction of philosophical critique. These scholars considered both the politics of anthropological representation and the politics of interpretation. They began to examine the epistemological assumptions held by pioneering anthropologists. Citing the texts of continental poststructuralists, they criticized ethnographic realism, in which anthropologists constructed societies as totalities. They delved into the moral implications that colonialist and neocolonialist politics held for the profession of anthropology. Confronting the postcolonial world with its incessant "heteroglossia," to borrow Bahktin's phrase, they questioned the bases of ethnographic authority.[12] The vast majority of this anthropological discourse on ethnographic authority is writing about writing, a corpus of criticism suggesting future directions in ethnographic expression. The number of anthropologists who have actually embedded these important issues in their ethnographies, however, is sadly limited. Of these ethnographies, several of the earliest are the most notable, especially Jean-Paul Dumont's thoughtful *The Headman and I* and Paul Riesman's incomparable *Freedom in Fulani Social Life.* In these and later texts, ethnographers worry, epistemologically speaking, about politics, representation, meaning(lessness), the dialectic of the ethnographer and the other, and the other's muted voice.[13] Several critics have complained of the interminable self-reflection, the theoretical anarchy, and the illocutionary opaqueness of these works.[14] Indeed, in his *Works and Lives* (1988) Clifford Geertz characterizes many of these anti-realist ethnographies as anemic, timid, and tirelessly self-doubting. Geertz notwithstanding, the writers of these books are, in Barthes's terms, attempting to write in the middle voice, writers who are attempting to take greater responsibility for the social and political ramifications of the words and images conveyed by their disseminated works.

Many of these ethnographies, however, are troubling. Despite the political and theoretical sensitivity of these "dead" authors, the writing in these works often reflects rather parochial dispositions. What are the social and political responsibilities of writing or filming social life? What does collaboration imply for written or filmed ethnography? Does one pay serious attention to non-Western theories of ethnographic authority? With the notable exception of the literature on indigenous media in visual anthropology,[15] these questions are usually left unanswered in the ethnographic literature.

One facile response to these quandaries is to suggest that questions of (ethnographic) authority are—but need not be —purely academic concerns. If the griots of Sahelian West Africa constitute a representative case, questions of authority are asked in many non-academic contexts and settings. Social context shapes the nature of the griot's performative discourse. Aesthetic convention influences the griot's performance styles. Like "dead" poets thrashed about in the winds of the postmodern condition, griots are more like writers in Barthes's sense. They are embodied intermediaries who creatively and respectfully use "old words" to reconstruct history and culture, to negotiate social identities, and to ruminate on stasis and change.[16]

Initially, there appear to be many affinities between griots and postmodern writers, but there are significant differences. Unlike Barthes's writer, whose subjectivity is overwhelmed by language, griots, who are also "owned" by language, are still able to use it to negotiate their multifaceted subjectivity. Griots are always implicated and embodied in their communities: they are full social and political participants in the villages where they live. Their words are performative: they help to create social life by talking it. For the most part, the words and images of postmodern writers are not performative. Most postmodern writers are shielded from the complicated negotiations of social life in other-land, which means that they are usually absolved from assuming an implicated—and embodied—responsibility for their words, images, and actions. Many contemporary writers are therefore disengaged and disembodied. By incorporating the griot's localized epistemology and practices into the more global representations of social science, scholars may be better able to produce works that meet the griot's greatest challenge: to express words and images that enable the dead to live again.[17]

Implication

Scholars, like griots, are implicated social actors in a field. In the words of French anthropologist Christine Bergé, "to be implicated means to be embroiled, compromised, entangled in an affair." Bergé does not limit her analysis of implication to a logical relationship; rather she sees the social interactional definition of implication as central to the scholarly enterprise. All human beings, even the most "objective" and "scientific" anthropologists, she says, are perforce implicated in a network of relationships.[18]

Although all human beings are "implicated" in Bergé's sense, anthropologists, according to her, are (over)implicated. The late French anthropologist Pierre Clastres, for example, considered his colleagues "Artaud functionaries."[19] The functionary is the representative of the establishment; he or she makes rules and follows them. Artaud is the illuminated wanderer, a nomad of the mind. In reality, anthropologists can never choose between Artaud and the functionary. As Bergé writes: "Even [Jacques] Lizot, [who lived for almost 20 participatory years among the Yanomami Indians] has his computer with him among the savages, and counts on his researcher's status. Publications assure him fame. One foot in France, one foot in the forest."[20]

One can say that the anthropologist is an over-implicated being, a crossroads of contradictory paths, a knot of unformulated desires. Like a . . . fragile retina, he views the world from a poorly received intimacy. He records speech, gestures, the distribution of elements, and exchanges and contributes to the transformation of values. He sometimes has a heart filled with repentance, a spirit filled with hope, and dirty, tired and trembling hands. Sometimes the anthropologist's body is sickened by this dismemberment. . . . Far from being a history of moral choice, implication is thus already the anthropologist's mode of existence.[21]

In the end, (over)implication in the field provokes a crisis during which scholars question the limits of the self, the illusion of unity, and the secret compromises of the real. As Bergé says philosophically, "Implication is the 'lived among.' It is the exercise of this reality: that there is not a position outside the system, that the anthropological gaze is not a 'gaze upon' but a sort of vibration on a fragile and ultra-sensitive antenna."[22]

Bergé's portrait of the (over)implicated scholar seems curiously similar to Barthes's "dead" author. Like the "dead" author, (over)implicated anthropologists relinquish their authority to the sweep of historical and contextual contingency. Like the "dead" author, the (over)implicated anthropologist becomes entranced by his or her contradictory path and is ultimately transformed into an intransitive medium whose subjectivity can be devoured by language.

To stop here, however, would not take us much beyond the anthropological writing of the 1980s. Despite its sensitivity,

Bergé's decidedly philosophical portrait of (over)implicated anthropologists leaves us muddled in scholarly practices in which (over)implicated writers are sometimes guilty of (over)-indulgence. Scholars certainly cannot deny their implication, even their (over)implication in a field. But if they focus attention on the griot's sensuous practices, might they not steer a middle course between the dead zones of scholarly intransitivity and transitivity? Given the contextual dynamics of their performances, it is clear that griots do not allow themselves to be completely devoured by language. They effortlessly negotiate the spaces between practice and theory, between sensible and intelligible. What can their practices teach us about the social scientist's consumption of other lives? What can their practices teach us about how other lives consume the social scientist?

Implication, Embodiment, and Voice

As noted in Chapter 1, Songhay people talk about implication through gustatory metaphors. People say, for example, that one person eats another and is in turn eaten by her or him—all part of the process of learning about social others. In Chapter 1, I noted that sorcerers eat a variety of pulverized plants to enhance their power, which enables them to "eat" (overpower) others. Such consumption, however, makes sorcerers vulnerable to a rival's insatiable appetite for power. For their part, Songhay griots say that they eat history and are eaten by it. Put another way, griots eat the "old words" and are eaten by them. In short, one consumes otherness in Songhay—in whatever form it takes—and is consumed, albeit partially, by otherness. In other words, one's implication in things Songhay can never be purely intellectual. For griots it means that the spoken word not only shapes and reshapes the story of the past, but is central to the negotiation and renegotiation of social roles in the present. The griot is never disengaged and disembodied. For scholars, this suggests acknowledging an embodied implication in our representations through (1) a critical awareness of the senses; (2) an attentiveness to voice; and (3) a recognition of the increasingly political implications of our works—a sensuous scholarship.

Most scholarship in anthropology and the other human sciences fails to follow the griot's first rule of practice: to create a dynamic tension between the poetic and the political, the past and the present. Most written and filmed ethnography, for example, is flat and analytic; it has often underplayed the importance of power relations in-the-world.[23] Such a discourse generates structures through dissection and categorization. Reacting to this dehumanizing process, the Senegalese novelist and filmmaker Sembène Ousmane, who considers himself a modern griot, once complained to French filmmaker Jean Rouch, "You observe us like insects."[24]

It would be too facile to suggest that the solution to the representational quandaries of depicting social life in the present is simply to adopt a more sensuous mode of scholarly expression. It would also be too simple to argue that the missing piece in the representational puzzle is that of voice. Writers search for their voices. Painters search for their styles—or so we are led to believe. Voice, of course, like writing and the concept of self, is not an element that exists in isolation. Scholars don't search for *voices*. As in the griot's case, historically and socially conditioned voices search for *them*. Sometimes, these voices find scholars and use their bodies to express the tension between the past and the present, the poetic and the political. Griots are at the center of a swirl of discordant voices, which they use creatively to craft their tales. The "old words" consume them, but not completely. So it is with scholars. Our voices cannot, strictly speaking, be our own. By the same token, the voices in scholary prose or documentary films cannot be strictly those of whom we represent. As David MacDougall points out, ethnographies sometimes take on a life of their own.[25] Sometimes scholars, like griots, shape what is presented to them to construct works that analyze and describe, evoke and provoke. In this way, scholars as griots become interlocutors in the ongoing conversation that constitutes social life.

The griot's talk, then, produces a cacophony of voices from past and present. What can scholars learn from this? The problem of voice is a central theme in many of Jean Rouch's films. Indeed, as I noted earlier, Rouch, who has participated in Songhay social life for more than fifty years, is considered a griot in the communities he films.[26] His long, implicated, and embodied exposure to others—Rouch calls it shared anthropology—has resulted in a rare and significant corpus of scholarly work. In such Rouch films as *Jaguar* (1967), *Moi, un noir* (1957), and *Petit à petit* (1969), one hears the distinct tones and articulations of many voices, including that of the filmmaker. And yet no one voice dominates these films. They constitute a corpus that is expressed not so much in Barthes's space of the intransitive middle voice as in a series of distinct voices in which subjectivity is not completely consumed by the immanence of language. In what remains of this chapter, I describe how the recognition and acceptance of my own long-term implication and embodiment in things Songhay impelled me to attempt to write ethnographies (*In Sorcery's Shadow* [1987, with Cheryl Olkes] and *Fusion of the Worlds* [1989]) in the manner of a griot.

Form and Voices in Ethnography

My implication in things Songhay has grown over a period of twenty years. During that time I have been a theory-testing anthropologist and a wide-eyed, naive apprentice to sorcerers. When, in 1979, a sorcerer in the town of Wanzerbé paralyzed me, I left the relative comforts of the Songhay social world and experienced for the first time the Songhay world of eternal war. I continued my apprenticeship in Songhay sorcery for several years. In 1984, however, when the world of eternal war became "too much with me," I renounced the Songhay path of power and, at the suggestion of my teacher, Adamu Jenitongo, opted for the Songhay path of plants—herbalism.

My immersion in this Songhay world, which is known to only a small number of Songhay sorcerers, posed many problems for me as a scholar. How could I write about my being poisoned or paralyzed? How could I describe the horrors and terrors of such a merciless world?

At first I tried to describe the world of Songhay sorcery in a disembodied language. I placed sorcery and witchcraft in a strictly theoretical context, and I described what happened to me in dispassionate, plain language. Although widely practiced, this tactic was unsatisfactory for me. I felt that such a "representation" of sorcery was a violation of the trust my teachers had placed in me. They had selected me to learn sorcery for two reasons: (a) they had seen a sign that I should be taught sorcerous secrets; and (b) they wanted someone entangled in their network to tell their story with dignity and respect. In short, they found in me an apprentice sorcerer and a griot. "We want you to take power objects from here and take them to America. We want you to make offerings to your altar in America. We also want you to tell our story, and tell it well—to bring us respect," they told me.

My griot's burden compelled me to write *In Sorcery's Shadow*, co-authored with Cheryl Olkes, more like a novel than an anthropological monograph, the latter usually consisting of, in the words of David Sapir, a theoretical introduction, a conclusion, and much Procrustean bedmaking in between.[27] We wanted readers to know my teachers as individuals who spoke in idiosyncratic ways. It is impossible to reproduce the zesty flavor of Songhay expressions in English translations, but one can attempt to add some Songhay spices to the translations, and one can certainly attempt to include in reconstructed dialogue the kinds of vocalizations that mark a particular speaker. But unlike Barthes's intransitive writer, we didn't want my subjectivity to be completely imprisoned by language. Rather, we wanted the pain, confusion, and euphoria of my experience to resonate for those who read about it. *In Sorcery's Shadow* includes musings about my feelings and reactions and reports on how others reacted to my existential dilemmas. As in the griot's performance, a number of voices are manipulated to shape my textual subjectivity. In short, the scholar's burden, the griot's burden, was to recreate the past—in my case the recent past—with sensuous delicacy and artistic verve. And so a way of writing *In Sorcery's Shadow* was chosen that evoked the sensuousness of the Songhay world, that homed in on the prosody of Songhay dialogue albeit translated into English, that caressed the texture of Songhay social relations. *In Sorcery's Shadow* is most certainly a personal take on my entanglement in Songhay sorcery, but in it the contentious voices of significant others are articulated. These efforts resulted in a book that poses many problems—personal, moral, and theoretical—and provides no answers. Readers are left to ponder these issues for themselves in the same way that members of Songhay audiences ponder the unanswered issues that griots articulate in their performances.

In West Africa griots are performers. Although the content of their genealogical and epic recitals must convey a certain number of key historical points in a prescribed historical style, there is much variation in griotic performances. The variation devolves from contextual factors. Who is in the audience? What is the occasion? Depending on audience and occasion, griots will edit their performances, emphasizing distant as opposed to recent history, singing at length about one particular branch of the royal family. The sociocultural context of performance, as we have seen, has a direct bearing on the "strategic" content of the griot's poetry.[28]

Just as the structure and content of the griot's poetry is sensitive to context, so the narrative strategy of the ethnographer's writing must not only be sensitive to audience but to distinct social settings. As in the griot's practice, the form and styles of ethnographic expression should vary with the subjects being described. So it is with *Fusion of the Worlds*, my ethnography of Songhay spirit possession, a text quite different from *In Sorcery's Shadow*. The world of Songhay sorcery is private, filled with resentments and jealousies. Songhay sorcerers do their "work" in the privacy of their houses late at night. The world of spirit possession is public, filled with music, movement, the flash of colors, and the acrobatics of the spirits in the bodies of mediums. Spirit possession ceremonies are carnivalesque, the combination of joyous festival and serious religious ritual. While the sorcerer confronts the sorcerous world alone, the diverse members of the Songhay spirit possession troupe (possession priests, mediums, praise-singers, musicians) confront the supernatural through the frame of a complex spirit pantheon.

The conditions that shaped the writing of *Fusion of the Worlds* were fundamentally different from those that textured the writing of *In Sorcery's Shadow*. The story of possession in Songhay is one of great complexity: hundreds of spirits, hundreds of spirit objects and costumes. It is also a story that cuts to the heart of Songhay social life: the complexity of social relations, the construction of gender idioms, the vicissitudes of agriculture in the Sahel, the symbolic re-creation of history. By the same token, the story of possession is a story of people: the personal pain of initiation, the social strains of mediumship, the interpersonal enmity that destroys social harmony in Songhay communities. How to portray such a tangled story in prose?

In *In Sorcery's Shadow* my entanglement in the Songhay world of sorcery devolved from confrontations with distinct individuals—other people in a limited network of sorcerous relations. Hence the memoir form of *In Sorcery's Shadow* conveyed, better than any other genre, the filigreed patterns of the Songhay world of sorcery. Since the world of Songhay possession is so much more complex, the simple storyline of *In Sorcery's Shadow* was incongruous. And so my struggle with the spirit possession material resulted in a multi-genre text, featuring narrative and multiple voices but also historical exposition and realist description. This maze of tones and voices are interconnected in the attempt to create, like the griot's complex performance, the seamless whole of an epic. And, like the griot's seamless epic, much of the burden of argument in *Fusion* is embedded in sensuous narrative rather than in the plain style exposition I have employed in this chapter.[29]

Fusion of the Worlds attempts to amplify a diversity of voices. My voices (anthropologist, griot, initiate) coexist with the voices of possession priests, spirit mediums, Songhay deities, and musicians as they tell their stories through a griotic re-creation of dialogue. Some of the voices of history are frozen in sober academic exposition, but others are juxtaposed with the blur of movement, the "cries" of the monochord violin, the clacks and rolls of the gourd drum, and the contours of spirit praise-poetry —other voices of history. The talk of the spirits and priests about the weather is adjoined to the detached observations of ecologists about monsoons: one hears about Dongo's (deity of thunder) path of rain as well as about the inter-tropical front. And, like the griot's talking social life, these diverse voices are arranged structurally to confront one another—always, to borrow James Fernandez's apt phrase, in an argument of images.[30] Why all this textual construction?

Ethnographies as Texts/Ethnographers as Griots

In 1982 George Marcus and Dick Cushman published their influential essay, "Ethnographies as Texts." This article defined a significant moment in anthropology; it forced anthropologists to confront themselves politically, epistemologically, and aesthetically. After "Ethnographies as Texts," anthropologists could no longer blithely "write up" their "data." Indeed, Marcus and Cushman had problematized the politics of ethnographic fieldwork as well as the politics of ethnographic writing. In the wake of "Ethnographies as Texts," there has been much published on ethnographic and representational practices.[31] In the wake of these latter reflections, there have been any number of essays in which writers are highly critical of what they call "postmodern" anthropology. For these writers, "postmodern" anthropology usually conflates—incorrectly I think—a cornucopia of analytical and textual approaches to the discipline (interpretive anthropology, reflexive ethnography, humanistic anthropology, narrative ethnography, post-Marxism, textualism, and so on). Some of these writers have berated what they term "the confused state of a new generation of American anthropologists."[32] Others complain about the hubris and careerism of so-called "postmodern" anthropologists.[33] Still others attempt to demonstrate the affinities among "postmodern" anthropology, parapsychology, and Shirley MacLaine![34]

These critics often dismiss the themes expressed in what they call postmodern works: social fragmentation, the loss of authority, the failure of social theory (challenges to positivism, empiricism, objectivism, comparative method, and inductive inquiry), and the onset of the hyperreal world of simulation. These themes, of course, did not appear out of thin air; they are linked inextricably to the condition of postmodernity brought on by the explosion and proliferation of high technology and the inexorable globalization of economic markets.[35] Even Kenneth Gergen, a social psychologist who unabashedly yearns for the "kinder" and "gentler" values of the romantic era, admits that postmodernity is here to stay, that postmodernity, like it or not, has not only reshaped the academy but inexorably changed our patterns of social relations.[36] Although it would be wonderful to return to the halcyon days of anthropology as an unquestioned science, the world has changed in fundamental ways. In these times it is essential for anthropologists and other social scientists to develop multifaceted epistemological and textual strategies that lend themselves to postmodern complexities. Otherwise, the world will pass us by and anthropology will become increasingly anachronistic.

There are, of course, no simple solutions to investigating, writing, or filming social life in the contemporary world. As

Rabinow long ago pointed out, the link between representation and politics can be fashioned with misleading facility.[37] Can one equate realism with colonialism? That, Rabinow argues, is too simple. Marcel Griaule and Michel Leiris, who held opposing views on colonialism, both wrote "realist" texts. Can narrative ethnography be equated with the textual contours of postcolonialism? Most of the texts loosely classed as postmodern have been preoccupied with the form and language of ethnography, which is reminiscent of the hermetic self-consciousness of high modernism—not postcolonialism—in the arts and literature.[38]

The beginning of postmodernity doesn't mean the end of ethnography. But it does force us to confront our practices anew and brings with it a chance to embrace with sensuous flexibility the aesthetic, epistemological, and political complexities of the contemporary world. Like a griot, Rabinow cautioned anthropologists about the problems of transparency in ethnographic writing and argued for an anthropological return to the world.[39] As griots well know, ethnographies can never be transparent; ethnographers "must face up to the fact that we can never avoid the author function."[40]

Rabinow's call for an anthropological return to the world is well advised. But we must leave the rarefied heights of textualism with our eyes wide open to complexity. "Postmodernism shares with hermeneutics a commitment to understanding culture and knowledge as socially constructed, but postmodernism is also committed to exploring the complex interrelationships between culture and power. It considers the genealogy of the cultural in terms of historically specific practices."[41] More specifically, Coombe suggests:

Postmodernism . . . is a perspective upon cultural practice that provokes us to consider phenomena in a new manner. It also suggests that we consider new phenomena, given the changing character of the worlds we live in. The historical sociocultural complex known as "the postmodern condition" or "the condition of postmodernity" refers to a multiplicity of processes . . . related to a global restructuring of capitalism, and new media, information and communications technologies.[42]

Coombe goes on to argue for what Said called "street savvy" ethnographies of everyday practices.[43] Everyday practices are complex, multifaceted, and creative. They demand a complex and multidimensional approach to ethnography. Ethnographies may be tales that ethnographers recount to readers or viewers, but the tales are no longer simple ones. They must now flexibly combine, as does the West African griot, history and economics, past and present, narrative and exposition. In *The Modernist City* James Holston calls for "critical ethnographies of modernism."[44] Rabinow's return to the world resulted in *French Modern*, in which the "author" mounts a critique of modernity through his analysis of a group of French colonial administrators who were urban planners during the 1920s. Rabinow has said that his book could be called "an ethnography of French pragmatic philosophical anthropology."[45] In both cases, these ethnographies focus more on sociocultural processes—the construction of discourse—than on how individuals or groups of individuals cope with the daily exigencies of contemporary life. For that, we need more sensuous texts—embodied, multi-genre constructions that combine narrative descriptions with historical and economic exposition. Boddy, Kondo, and Narayan, for example, have all constructed elegant texts that integrate narrative and exposition, individual and social, and local and global perspectives through cultural analyses of gender, identity, and politics.[46]

It takes a lifetime for griots to shape their delicately embodied ethnographic performances. For scholars, nothing is more difficult than crafting a multigenre text. What threads can one weave through the text to make its disparate elements hang together? How does one juxtapose exposition, dialogue, and narrative? How does one develop a sense of place—that is, of locality—in scholarly expression? These questions are answered only when social scientists struggle with their complex materials.

And yet, no one investigates, writes or films social life in isolation. The persistent ethical and political questions remain. Why do we write? For whom? When asked these questions about his films, French anthropologist and filmmaker Jean Rouch replied. "First, I make films for myself. Second, I make films for the people whom I film. Third, I make films for general audiences."[47] Rouch's answer brings us back to the griot. The griot's tongue never articulates social life in isolation. Griots talk social life for themselves, for their communities, and increasingly, for general audiences. Griots must confront their fluid "materials"

—the ever-changing complexities of contemporary social life— before, during, and after their performances. The griot's tongue must remain flexible.

Scores of social scientists, literary critics, and philosophers will no doubt continue their stimulating debates about voice, difference, reflexivity, representation, the phenomenology of the field encounter, and the politics of both interpretation and publication. Such critical debate expands the space in which issues of representation are debated. But can we afford to ignore the griot's examples? Standing on the griot's spot, which is marked by contested history and cultural politics, scholars are charged with the burden of transforming the griot's multi-faceted practices into expression. This responsibility means that scholars seek ways of sensuously investigating, writing, and filming social life that enable the dead to live again and the living to recognize better ways of coping with the confusions of contemporary life. Is this not a burden worthy of future efforts to dwell in the embodied power of history?

PART 2
BODY AND MEMORY

Introduction: The Texture of Memory

In Part One we saw how sensuous localized epistemologies shape cultural practices among the Songhay people of the Republic of Niger. Songhay sorcerers eat power—in the form of what they call *kusu*—which can both empower and overpower their bodies. Songhay griots eat history and as a consequence are "owned" by the "old words" they have ingested. In Part Two, the chapters suggest that embodied processes—the construction and reconstruction of local epistemologies—spark cultural memories.

To use the language of Paul Connerton, flesh both *inscribes* and *incorporates* cultural memory and history.[1] These memories may take the form of a scar that recalls a tortuous episode. They may be triggered by the stylized movements of dance, the melodic contours of music, the fragrant odors of perfume, or, perhaps, the rhapsody of song. Usually these sensuous modalities provoke memories—and histories—"from below," histories of the dispossessed that historians never recorded. These are memories of existential content: pain, hunger, abuse, struggle, mirth, pleasure—the very substance of a sensuous scholarship. As such, the elicitation and presentation of embodied cultural memories fleshes out the story of a people. In this way scholars are able to explore the multifaceted textures of memory, which can profoundly humanize our reconstructions of the past.

Embodied cultural memories, however, do not constitute a thorough exploration of memory or history. For that, one needs to combine text and body, analysis and sensibility. In the chapters of Part Two, I attempt to achieve this scholarly balance. Chapter 3, "Embodying Colonial Memories," argues that spirit possession among the Songhay peoples is a theater of embodied cultural memory in which fundamental existential themes are presented and re-presented through odor, sound, movement. Chapter 4, "'Conscious' Ain't Consciousness," considers how the senses order and re-order cultural memory. In both chapters, I suggest how and why a more sensuous approach to scholarship might expand and improve scholarly investigations of the past.

3
EMBODYING COLONIAL MEMORIES

The acrid smell of burning resins wafts through Adamu Jenitongo's compound, preparing it for the *holle* (spirits). It is late
afternoon in Tillaberi, and the sounds of a Songhay spirit
possession ceremony crackle through the dusty air: the high
pitched "cries" of the monochord violin, the resonant clacks of
bamboo drumsticks striking gourd drums, the melodious contours of the praise-singer's "old words," the patter of dancing
feet on dune sand.

It is a white hot day in June 1987, and the mix of sounds
and smells brings the spirits to Adamu Jenitongo's egg-shaped
dunetop compound. Four mudbrick houses shimmer in the
languorous heat. From under a thatched canopy at the compound entrance, the orchestra continues to play spirit music.
The spirits like Adamu Jenitongo's compound. Drawn by pungent smells, pulsing sounds and dazzling dance, they visit it day
and night. On this day the *Gengi Bi*, or spirits of the earth,
have already come to the compound to bless members of the
audience, giving them the courage to confront their hunger
and sicknesses. They sing rather than talk, and their mysterious
melodies have lingered and dissipated into the dusky air.

They are not the only visitors on this day. Clustered in front of
the musician's canopy are three Hauka spirits—spirits of European force. They groan, bellow, and thump their chests with
clenched fists as they stamp across the sand. Saliva bubbles from
their mouths. They babble. Their eyes blaze.

Istambula, the leader of the Hauka, is there, as is General
Malia, the General of the Red Sea. These "military" officers are
served well by Bambara Mossi, a conscripted foot soldier who
is exceedingly crass. "Hauk'ize," Istambula shouts. "Hauk'ize of
Tillaberi, present yourselves for our Roundtable," he says in
Songhay. Slowly the non-possessed men and women who carry

Hauka spirits form a loose circle around the deities. Bambara Mossi makes sure that the mediums stand at "attention" in the presence of Istambula and General Malia.

Adamu Jenitongo and the anthropologist are seated under the shade of a tall eucalyptus, the unquenchable thirst of which has withered the other trees in the compound. They sit silently on palm frond mats and swat flies. The Hauka Roundtable is about to convene. Suddenly Istambula breaks through the circle of mediums and runs stiff-legged in the direction of Jenitongo and the anthropologist. He leaves his feet like a swan diver and belly flops just in front of them.

"I swear to Bonji (God). I swear to Bonji," he mutters in Pidgin French, "that . . . that you go come wit' us." Standing in the shadows of the canopy, the Hauka mediums look toward Jenitongo and the anthropologist. "You must join us," Istambula says switching to Songhay. "We need your words."

Although Istambula's glowing eyes peer into the anthropologist's, he must be talking about the anthropologist's mentor, Adamu Jenitongo, the wisest and most powerful man in the region.

"We need your words," Istambula repeats in Songhay. "In the name of Bonji."

Adamu Jenitongo says nothing.

Mounkaila, a tall wiry man, waves to the anthropologist from the canopy. "Hey, Anasaara (European) hey," he states in Songhay. "He wants you. Come!"

"Me?" the anthropologist asks.

Mounkaila beckons him to join the circle.

Meanwhile Istambula's inert body, stinking of sweat and dirt, is jolted with what seem to be electroshocks. His face crinkles like burning paper as he pushes himself up on one knee and lifts his right hand toward the anthropologist. "We go jus'now." he says in Pidgin. "We need your words," he says in Songhay.

"Why me?" the anthropologist asks in Songhay.

"I European. You European. We European." he says in Pidgin. "You hear me?"

Adamu Jenitongo tells the anthropologist to stand up. He extends his hand to Istambula, who grabs it and pulls himself up. Braced against the anthropologist's shoulder, Istambula staggers over to the canopy to resume his place at the center of the

Figure 4. Hauka Spirit Possession, Tillaberi, Niger, 1977.

group. Mounkaila puts his hand on the anthropologist's shoulder.

"Thank you for coming to our discussion. It is only correct that all the Europeans in Tillaberi attend the meeting. That, of course, includes you," he concludes.

"Thanks," the anthropologist says nervously.

The General braces himself against one of the non-possessed Hauka mediums. He breathes heavily. His limbs move stiffly, robotically. "We must listen, now. There is talk that one of you must be straightened out. Who is on trial here?"

Mounkaila answers in Pidgin. "He no de, Mon General."

The General erupts. "Why didn't he come?"

"He is ashamed," answers another of the Hauka mediums.

"Anasaara," the General says to the anthropologist in Songhay, "what do you think? Should he be here to account for what he has done?"

The anthropologist, of course, doesn't know the identity of the offender. But, having played this game many times before, he answers. "Of course, he should be here."

Istambula chimes in. "Hauk'ize. You know that we demand an oath," he begins in Songhay. "You mus' waka wit' Bonji," he follows in Pidgin. "You must obey the rules," he says switching back to Songhay. "When we choose you, we give you force, and you must not abuse your power." He pounds his chest. "I Istambula. Istambula, do you hear?" You go hear me, Hauk'ize?"

Bracing himself against Mounkaila, Istambula brings his contorted visage a few inches from the anthropologist's and sprays saliva in his face. "One of the Hauk'ize has had relations with his friend's wife," he says in Songhay. "Do you hear, Anasaara? Do you hear?" He swings away from the white man and Mounkaila, twirling in the center of the circle. "Do you hear, Hauk'ize? Relations with his friend's wife. No discipline. What is to be done with him?"

Bambara Mossi slaps his massive chest with a hardwood baton. "I go cut off, dangela," he says in Pidgin French. "I go get knife. I go cut 'im fas' fas'."

Laughter explodes at the Roundtable. "Non," says General Malia in Pidgin. "He go tek white chicken an' kill 'im fo' bus'."

Islambula nods. "Hauk'ize," he shouts. "Hauk'ize. I testify to

Bonji and to Dongo, father of us all. The General has a good idea. You must go to this man's house and tell him. You must tell him to take a white chicken and go to my altar in the bush."

Mounkaila, who has become Istambula's spokesperson, repeats the deity's words.

"This particular person must go there," says Istambula, "do you hear me . . . he must go there on Saturday. And all the Hauk'ize must go with him." Istambula switches into Pidgin. "I Istambula. I go bak Malia now. I go bak."

In response to Istambula's statements, the musicians raise the tempo. The pulsations ripple like waves through Istambula's body. He extends his arms and spins around like a top. He grunts and howls. Saliva flows like lava from his mouth. Bambara Mossi and General Malia join him. The tempo is quite fast; the beat is intense. One by one the Hauka throw their bodies in the air, landing on their backs with thumps. They lie there on the dune like sacks of millet at market—heavy, motionless, and unconscious. Finally liberated from their Hauka, the mediums cough, slowly sit up, and dust themselves off. Attendants bring them water.

*   *   *

The body of an African medium is possessed by a "European" deity who presides over a Roundtable discussion in which the views of Africans and other "Europeans" are expressed in a mixture of Pidgin French and Songhay. The Roundtable is a remarkable public forum during which Istambula, the chief of the Hauka (Songhay spirits that burlesque European colonial personages) even invites the participation of the European "occupying" the body of an anthropologist. The problem under discussion—a Hauka medium's sexual transgression—is debated and resolved. The Hauka, who are curiously horrific, comedic, and dignified, have come and gone. By resolving yet another social problem in Tillaberi, they have reinforced their authority. Like the French colonial army of many years past, the Hauka are seen as powerful political beings: they get things done quickly, efficiently. Most Songhay consider efficiency a "European" trait.

Embodiment and Spirit Possession

Most people know the Hauka only through the shocking images of Jean Rouch's monumental film *Les maîtres fous*, in which possessed black men are portrayed as rabid "dogs" who shamelessly chomp on boiled dog meat—a kind of voyeuristic colonial cannibalism. In my view the images of *Les maîtres fous* are the cinematic equivalent of Artaud's Theater of Cruelty, in which images move us beyond the anesthetizing influence of language to an uncompromising confrontation with the culturally repressed dimensions of our being (see Chapter 6). But the existential power of these images doesn't give viewers much ethnographic information about the Hauka.[1] Viewers learn little about the history or the social context of the Hauka movement. They learn still less about the social power of the Hauka, a power that has grown with time. Jean Rouch has written about the Hauka in his untranslated *Migrations au Ghana*, but only tangentially.[2] Historians such as Finn Fugelstad have written essays that describe the early moments of the Hauka movement as cultural resistance to French colonialism.[3] My own writing on the Hauka has included (a) discussions of the history and evolution of the Hauka from colonial times to the present; (b) considerations of the political power of the Hauka, especially following Nigerien independence; and (c) critical assessments of Jean Rouch's films, including, of course, *Les maîtres fous*.[4]

The Hauka movement is a particularly compelling example of spirit possession, a subject with an extensive literature in anthropology, sociology, and religious studies. Like most previous writing on the phenomenon of spirit possession, the disquisitions on the Hauka have generally overlooked one fundamental point: that spirit possession is fundamentally an embodied phenomenon. There can be little doubt that the body is the focus of possession phenomena. Whether writers call it trance or possession, the same dramatic process presents itself cross-culturally. Musicians, praise-singers, and priests use a variety of expressive media to entice spirits (external forces) to leave non-human realms and enter human bodies. In so doing, the spirit enters social space, transforming mediums both physically and symbolically. Much has been written about the medium's sym-

Figure 5. A medium possessed by the Hauka, Istambula, Tillaberi, Niger, 1984.

bolic transformation and the "texts" he or she expresses.[5] Much less has been written about the bodily experience of possession.

In this chapter, I argue that embodiment is not primarily textual; rather, the sentient body is culturally consumed by a world filled with forces, smells, textures, sights, sounds, and tastes, all of which trigger cultural memories.[6]

Hauka spirit possession is simultaneously frightening and funny. Elsewhere I have referred to Hauka spirit possession as "horrific comedy."[7] The horrific/comedic embodiment of the Hauka and its mimetic connection to colonial memories evokes the past, manipulates the present, and provokes the future. Through the power of embodiment the Hauka stutter-step over the border separating ritual from political practice. In the Republic of Niger, spirit possession is a set of embodied practices that constitutes power-in-the-world. Diplomacy on the dune informs diplomacy in the Presidential Palace.

Sensing Spirit Possession

Vision, as I suggested in Part One of this book, has governed perception in Western metaphysics.[8] Accordingly, the guiding metaphors of the humanities and social sciences have been visual ones: infrastructures and superstructures, systems and configurations, texts and metatexts. Throughout the history of anthropology, ethnographers have been participant *observers* who *reflect* on their *visual* experiences and then write *texts* that *represent* the Other's *pattern* of kinship, exchange, or religion.

The ethnographic study of spirit possession is no exception. Theories of spirit possession spatialize the phenomenon in any number of ways. Possession is grafted to social structures or is *seen* as a set of texts that constitute a counterhegemonic discourse. Anthropologists have long used "data" on spirit possession to expound on theories of society or of social meaning. Writers have employed five dominant forms of explanation to analyze spirit possession: functionalist, psychoanalytic, physiological, symbolic (interpretive/textual), and theatrical.[9] Each of these orientations has its particular strengths, but no theory in my opinion adequately captures the sociocultural, historical, and political nuances of spirit possession. My argument in this chapter is that although the major theorists on spirit possession make significant contributions to social theory, they fail to consider sufficiently (a) the centrality of the sentient body in possession, (b) the relationship between bodily practices (spirit possession) and cultural memory, and (c) the political power that devolves from embodiment. By considering spirit possession sensuously as an embodied practice, I suggest, we are likely to sense it as a phenomenological arena in which cultural memory is fashioned and refashioned to produce and reproduce power.

Spirit Possession and the Body

As mentioned in the Prologue, a spate of recent articles, anthologies, and monographs have analyzed the centrality of the body in social theory. Feminist and poststructuralist scholars, among others, have vigorously critiqued the Cartesian split between mind and body. I have also stressed that in anthropology it is important to consider the body's sensuousness, especially in those societies in which textualism is not central. In Songhay, for example, spirits must be enticed to their social bodies through music (sound), praise-poetry (sound), specific perfumes (smell), and dance (movement). Once the medium has abandoned her or his body to a deity, what happens? In a remarkable passage, Rouch describes the sentient embodiment that occurs in Songhay possession.

> Following numerous indirect accounts [it is already indicated that the dancer must not remember the possession] the dancer *sees* the spirit [eventually the old initiates see it too] penetrate the dance circle and direct itself toward him or her; the spirit holds in its hands the skin of a freshly slaughtered animal and presents the bloody side of it to the dancer three times:
> —the first time, tears flow from the dancer's eyes;
> —the second time, mucus flows from the dancer's nose;
> —the third time, the dancer cries out.[10]

On its fourth pass, the spirit places the bloody skin over the dancer's head. In this way the spirit captures the medium's double and enters the dancer's body. During spirit possession, the dancer's double is protected under the bloody skin. When the spirit leaves the body, it lifts off the bloody animal skin, liberating the dancer's double. The medium opens his or her eyes. Sometimes mediums, like those in Tillaberi who carried Istambula, General Malia, and Bambara Mossi, remain unconscious for several minutes. They always cough as if they had just left an airless vault.[11]

Why is it important to home in on the sentient body of the spirit medium? The answer is deceptively simple: the body is a major repository of cultural memories—memories, to quote Toni Morrison, "of the flesh."

Spirit Possession and Cultural Memory

The overwhelming tendency to consider spirit possession ceremonies as discourse or as expressions of social affliction has two major theoretical consequences. The first is that many studies of spirit possession fail to consider its relation to history. The second is that discursive analysis (possession as text) as opposed to sensory analysis (possession as bodily practice) unwittingly underscores the mind/body split in the academy.

In his *How Societies Remember* (1989) Paul Connerton wonders how the collective memory of groups is expressed and sustained. He demonstrates that ceremonies like spirit possession, among others, are more than sites of consciousness-raising about gender relations, more than arenas in which anti-colonialist discourses are constructed.

If there is such a thing as social memory . . . we are likely to find it in commemorative ceremonies; but commemorative ceremonies prove to be commemorative only in so far as they are performative; performativity cannot be thought without a concept of habit; and habit cannot be thought without a notion of bodily automatisms.[12]

Connerton distinguishes three types of memory: personal, cognitive, and habit. The first two types have been studied extensively. Psychoanalysts have focused on the personal memory of one's life history. Psychologists have probed cognitive memory, which concerns our ability to recall certain external facts, stories, words, the meaning of a poem or short story—all of which is part of the attempt to delimit universal cognitive structures. Little attention has been focused on Connerton's third category of memory, habit-memory, which Connerton defines as "having the capacity to reproduce a certain performance."[13] Habit is something which does not lend itself to the visual bias that is central to discursive analysis. In their insistence on the discursive, scholars transform the figurative into language and text—into discourse. And yet our memories are never purely personal, purely cognitive, or purely textual. Citing Maurice

Halbwachs, Connerton argues that the analytical separation of individual and social memory is meaningless. To consider the formation of social memory, it follows that one must consider how those memories are constructed and conveyed through such commemorative ceremonies as spirit possession.

What is it about these commemorative ceremonies that triggers collective cultural memory? Connerton suggests a number of factors:

1. Ritual is performative in the sense of Austin's notion of the performative utterance.[14] That is, performatives constitute rather than reflect action.
2. Ritual is formal in the sense that its structure and content are conservative and repetitive.

According to Connerton, both factors are mnemonic. In addition, performatives are not limited to verbal utterances; they are also "encoded in set postures, gestures and movements."[15] All rituals are constituted by performativity and formalism. But commemorative rituals have one additional feature that sets them apart; they "explicitly refer to mnemonic persons and events, whether these are understood to have a historical or a mythological existence"[16]; they are ritual re-enactments.

Up to this point, Connerton's argument is hardly innovative. Anthropologists taking the perspective championed by Victor Turner have long analyzed ritual in a similar manner. Two elements, however, distinguish Connerton's analysis of commemorative ritual. First, unlike most symbolic anthropologists, Connerton's focus is decidedly historical; it is also embodied.

A ritual is not a journal or memoir. Its master narrative is more than a story told and reflected on; it is a cult enacted. An image of the past, even in the form of a master narrative, is conveyed and sustained by ritual performances. And this means that what is remembered in commemorative ceremonies is something in addition to a collectively organized variant of personal or cognitive memory. For if ceremonies are to work for their participants, if they are to be persuasive to them, then those participants must not be simply cognitively competent to execute the performance; they must be habituated to those performances. This habituation is to be found . . . in the bodily substrate of the performance.[17]

In the last part of his book, Connerton demonstrates how bodily practices—the embodied substrate of performance—key cultural memory. In cultural memory, "the past is, as it were, sedimented in the body."[18] The process of sedimentation occurs through two kinds of practices: inscription and incorporation. Inscribing practices refer to the storage and retrieval of texts in photographs, books, audio cassettes, video cassettes, the cinema. Incorporating practices refer to body postures, gestures, facial expressions, body movements, table manners.

Most scholars of social phenomena have privileged practices of inscription; they can be analyzed discursively as texts, a metaphor that has even been extended to cultural markings on the body. Such is the focus of cultural hermeneutics from Schleiermacher to Ricoeur. "Inscriptions, and hence texts, were privileged objects of interpretation because the activity of interpretation itself became an object of reflection, rather than being simply practiced, in a particular context."[19] Which is why hermeneutical analysis is so well suited to the study of Western culture—a culture of texts and textual analysis. Connerton is correct in asserting that scholars should pay more attention to what he calls incorporating practices, which in this book I term embodiment. If we are to comprehend ritual in non-western settings, we need to juxtapose text to body. This point is especially important in the analysis of non-Western commemorative rituals in which scholars all too often inscribe the body. That the body is inscribed is uncontestable, but to stop there is a serious epistemological error, for in its textualization the body, as I have argued in this book, is robbed of its movements, odors, tastes, sounds—its sensuousness, all of which are potent conveyors of meaning and memory.

Considering embodiment, in fact, becomes central in the analysis of what George Lipsitz calls "counter-memory."[20] Some critics would call counter-memory a subaltern discourse. In her major study of zar spirit possession in northern Sudan, Janice Boddy refers to it as counterhegemonic and a subversive discourse.[21] Social scientists and literary critics approach counter-memory through the analysis of texts or events (like spirit possession) as texts. In his consideration of counter-memory, Lipsitz looks to artistic rather than scholarly expression, to

the novels of authors from the cultural margins: women and
men from non-mainstream groups (such as Toni Morrison, and
Leslie Silko). In these groups, memories were more likely to be
stored in tales, objects and bodies than in texts. Toni Morrison
articulates this point eloquently.

You know, they straightened out the Mississippi River in places, to
make room for houses and livable acreage. Occasionally the river
floods these places. "Floods" is the word they use, but in fact it is not
flooding; it is remembering. Remembering where it used to be. All
water has a perfect memory and is forever trying to get back where it
was. Writers are like that: remembering where we were, what valley we
ran through, what the banks were like, the light that was there and the
route back to our original place. It is emotional memory—where the
nerves and the skin remember how it appeared. And a rush of imagination is our "flooding."²²

Writings like Morrison's *Beloved*, according to Lipsitz and
others, mount a fundamental challenge to history's reliance
on inscription.²³ Gayl Jones's novel *Corregidora* (see Chapter 4) is a case in point. In this haunting tale about cultural
memory and the counter-memory of four generations of Afro-
Brazilian and African American women, the protagonist's great-
grandmother's refrain is

The important thing is making generations. They can burn the papers
but they can't burn conscious, Ursa. And that's what makes the evidence. And that's what makes the verdict.²⁴

In this tale, the evidence is sedimented in the bodies of black
women, all of whom are haunted by the hulking presence of
a Portuguese sailor who settled in Brazil and then in Louisi-
ana. Old Man Corregidora fed his lust by buying and pos-
sessing beautiful black women, including the women of Ursa's
family. According to documents, Corregidora had legitimately
employed these slaves; the documents make no mention of his
whoring, pimping, and incestuous rages. But the heart of the
story—the counter-memory—tells a different tale: one of sexual
slavery, of the persistent memories of physical and emotional
abuse and incest. Even Ursa and her mother, neither of whom
had ever known Corregidora, were haunted by his presence.
His hulking image torments their collective cultural memory,

itself constituted by the invisible history of male sexual abuse. The following passage dramatically exemplifies cultural memory as a fundamentally embodied phenomenon.

The two women in that house. The three of them at first and then when I was older, just the two of them, one sitting in a rocker, the other in a straight-back chair, telling me things. I'd always listen. I never saw my mama with a man, never ever saw her with a man. But she wasn't a virgin because of me. And still she was heavy with virginity. Her swollen belly with no child inside. And still she never had a man. Or never let me see her with one. No, I think she never had one. . . . When I was real little, Great Gram rocking me and talking. And still it was as if my mother's whole body shook with that first birth and memories and she wouldn't make others and she wouldn't give those to me, though she passed the other ones down, the monstrous ones, but she wouldn't give her own terrible ones. Loneliness. I could feel it, like she was breathing it, like it was all in the air. Desire, too. I couldn't recognize it then. But now when I look back, that's all I see. Desire, and loneliness. A man that left her. Still she carried their evidence, screaming, fury in her eyes.[25]

But the memories of abuse and abandonment extend well beyond those of Ursa's mother and her pre-ordained fate with men. The fury and sadness also infused Ursa's voice, especially when she sang the blues at Happy's Club.

What Gayl Jones is telling us between the lines of her eloquent prose is that the power of collective memory does not merely devolve from textual inscriptions. It stems from stories (the oral tradition). It also emerges from somewhere behind the eyes. It is squeezed from the sound-pain of the blues. For Gayl Jones, collective memory is derived from sentiments so elemental that they are beyond words. When Ursa sings the blues, she is possessed by the spirit of cultural memory. Her singing is therefore body-felt, a fact that her audience appreciates.

Connerton's theoretical designs fit spirit possession like a glove. Spirit Possession is a commemorative ritual in which bodily practices (gestures, sounds, postures, and movements) are never minimized. For her part, Jones's literary evocation of collective memory brings us closer to a sensuous theory of spirit possession in which embodied practices—beyond the text— give us an opening to indigenous historiographic practice.

Embodiment, Cultural Memory, and
Songhay Spirit Possession

Among the Songhay peoples of Niger and Mali, spirit possession has a long history. Olivier de Sardan traces the origin of
possession to the late fifteenth century, a time when Islam was
institutionalized during the reign of Askia Mohammed Touré.[26]
Each spirit family in the Songhay pantheon—there are six of
them—represents a particular period in Songhay history. The
Tooru represent the earliest and most powerful Songhay ancestors who founded the first Songhay dynasty—the Zas. The *Genji
Kwaari* or white spirits are Muslim clerics who became important during the reign of Askia Mohammed. The *Genji Bi* or black
spirits represent the first inhabitants of Songhay—the masters
of the land. The *Doguwa* or Hausa spirits are of a much more
recent vintage. They came into the Songhay pantheon around
1911 during a vast migration of Hausa-speaking peoples into
Songhay. The Hauka are the spirits of colonization and date to
1925.

Based on the parallel expansions of dominance, experience
and spirit families, one could argue that Songhay spirit possession constitutes a "discourse" on history. That would be both
facile and specious. There are three paths to the constitution
and reconstitution of Songhay history: the written tradition, the
oral tradition, and the performance of spirit possession ceremonies. The first path is that of written history. Unlike the
situation for many groups in West Africa, there is a long Songhay textual tradition. Two historical documents stand out: es-
Sadi's *Tarikh es-Soudan* (collected and written in the seventeenth
century) and Kati's *Tarikh al Fattach* (written in the sixteenth
century).[27] These histories of the Songhay Empire (1463–1591)
document a sanitized (Islamized) version of the Songhay past.
They are virtually unknown in Mali and Niger.

The second path is that of the oral tradition. As for other
groups in the Sahel, there is a longstanding epic tradition in
Songhay. The griot has long been the oral historian, the custo-
dian of tales that speak to the greatness of Empire, the valor
of past battles, the courage of past kings. Whereas the *Tarikh*
are whitewashed testaments to the Muslim purity of imperial
Songhay, the oral tradition speaks to the non-Islamic magical

capacities of Songhay kings.[28] But the *Epic of Askia Mohammed* is hardly what Lipsitz would call a literary vehicle for Songhay counter-memory. The epics have always been performed, which means that their structures are invariable; the content, however, varies with the social politics of the performance context. In addition, the epics are stories about the glories of the Songhay elite; they do not reflect the existential struggles of families of Songhay farmers.[29] Although elements of the epics are known to many people in Songhay, they trigger only flashes of Songhay cultural memory. They do not constitute a counter-memory. They do not speak to the elemental aspects of Songhay experience in the world. For that, we need to consider the third path to Songhay history: spirit possession.

The way of the text and the epic are decidedly disembodied paths to Songhay history, which constrains their messages. The text and the epic speak to aspects of Songhay memory. Spirit possession ceremonies spark Songhay counter-memories, which are, as we have seen, stored in movement, in posture, in gestures, in sound, odor, and tastes—in the flesh. Whereas the text and the epic speak to the consciousness of the nobility, the bodily practices of possession speak to what Ursa's Great Gram called "conscious."

Songhay spirit possession is a sensory arena of counter-memory. The performance of spirit possession ceremonies reenacts, to borrow Connerton's phrase, the experience of the Songhay. The Songhay say that the monochord violin "cries" (*heh*); its "cries" cut to the heart of Songhay. As the "cries" of the violin enter the bodies of both mediums and spectators, the music, according to my teachers, resonates existential themes: the powerlessness of the human confrontation with nature; the utter contingency of life in the Sahel; the delicate balance between life and death; the unresolved tensions between men and women, old and young, friends and foes. These are historical themes of struggle, of perseverance in a hot, drought-plagued land, of resignation—even the nobles bear powerless witness to the ravages of nature in the Sahel. These themes, the very substance of counter-memory, are rarely found in historical texts or in epics.

*   *   *

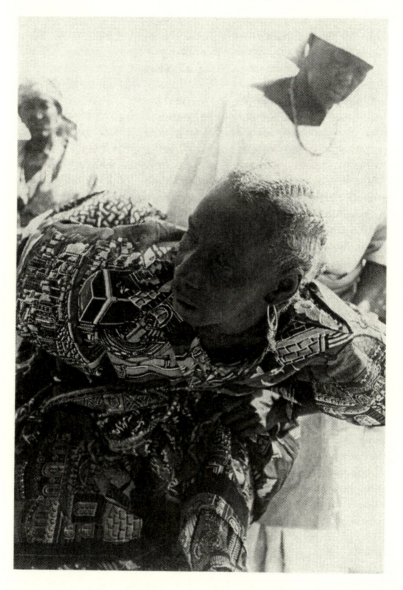

Figure 6. A medium embodies cultural memory, Djomona, Niger, 1977.

And so cultural memories are embedded in the smells, sounds, and sights of Songhay spirit possession ceremonies. In a blur of movement, the various dance steps of Songhay possession recount the journey of the spirits from water to heavens and back to earth. But there is more still. Aside from smelling and hearing the past, spectators also see the faces of old women dancing, faces creased and folded by their gritty lives in the Sahel. The frail old women dance, their movements in sync with the quickening pace of the music. They dance and dance until one sees smiles so radiant that they wash from those old faces years of sun and hard work. Those smiles speak to pride and power, for these women know—as do members of the audience—that without their bodies, which they lend to the spirits, there would be no spirit possession in Songhay, no protection from the ravages of nature.

Embodied Memories: Mimesis and Spirit Possession

So far, I have argued that spirit possession is an incontestably embodied phenomenon that triggers myriad cultural memories. Such a proposition, however, recounts only part of a sensuous tale. How can we explain the power of spirit possession to evoke the past, manipulate the present, and provoke the future? How can we explain the power of spirit possession to shape both local and state politics? My tentative answer is that spirit possession is an arena of sensuous mimetic production and reproduction, which makes it a stage for the production and reproduction of power.

Michael Taussig is one scholar who believes that human perception is fundamentally sensuous.

> Like Adorno and Benjamin . . . my concern is to reinstate in and against the myth of Enlightenment, with its universal, context free reason, not merely the resistance of the concrete particular to abstraction, but what I deem crucial to thought that moves and moves us—namely its sensuousness, its mimeticity.[30]

In his 1993 book, *Mimesis and Alterity,* Taussig links sensuous perception to the power of mimesis, the capacity to copy perceived reality—and its relationship to alterity, the process of socially constructing otherness. Taussig takes as his problem the presence of curing figurines among the Cuna Indians of San Blas, Panama. Curiously, the figures depict colonial Europeans. Why would figurines of such intrinsic importance to Cuna healing rites take the form of colonial Europeans? From his vantage as a "European type," Taussig wonders: "What magic lies in this, my wooden self, sung to power in a language I cannot understand?"[31]

This magic, in Taussig's analysis, cuts to the very heart of the anthropological enterprise:

For if I take these figurines seriously, it seems that I am honor-bound to respond to the mimicry of my-self in ways other than the defensive maneuver of the powerful by subjecting it to scrutiny as yet another primitive artifact, grist to the analytic machinery of Euroamerican anthropology. The very mimicry corrodes the alterity by which my science is nourished. For now I too am part of the object of study. The Indians have made me alter to my self.[32]

The problem of the Cuna figurines leads Taussig into a wondrous maze of paradoxes. The Cuna say that the figurines consist of two aspects: inner and outer. It is from the intangible inner aspect that healing power is derived. This ethnographic fact compels Taussig to ask why the figurines take the form of Europeans. "Why bother carving forms at all if the magical power is invested in the spirit of the wood itself? And indeed, as our puzzling leads to more puzzling, why is embodiment itself necessary?"[33]

Walter Benjamin provides Taussig a provisional answer. "The ability to mime, and mime well . . . is the capacity to Other."[34] Through this capacity—what Taussig calls the "mimetic faculty" —one is able to grasp that which is strange—other—through resemblances, through copies of it. The power of the mimetic faculty devolves from its fundamental sensuality: miming something entails contact. Copying a thing, even a European type, is (electro)shocking; it creates a flash of sensation that engenders a sense of comprehension, mastery. For Benjamin and Taussig, knowing is corporeal. One mimes to understand. We copy the world to comprehend it through our bodies.[35]

Recognition, it follows, is an embodied phenomenon that is part and parcel of the mimetic faculty. Through the embodied displacement of the self, recognition strikes us in a flash. Here Taussig cites Benjamin: "The past can be seized only as an image which flashes up at an instant when it can be recognized and is never seen again."[36]

These sensuous mimetic processes, Taussig notes, are very much at work in magic. Sympathetic magic consists of copy and contact. Sorcerers make a copy of what they want to affect. Through its magical power the copy acquires the properties of the original, which in turn implies the sorcerer's mastery and power over the object. Songhay sorcerers, for example, sometimes make copies of magic arrows and bows associated with the arrows and bow of a particular spirit in the Songhay pantheon. On rare occasions they will speak to these replicas from their hearts, naming a victim. Then they take the bow and shoot the arrow in the direction of the victim's dwelling or village. The replica falls harmlessly on the ground in the sorcerer's compound, but the "inner" arrow flies through the night air. And if a sorcerer's aim is good—if the power pulsing in his veins is greater than that of his enemy/victim—the "inner" arrow strikes its target. Victims will wake up in the middle of the night, screaming with a pain that short-circuits up their legs. Once struck, they become progressively weaker. And if they don't seek a cure, they will most certainly die from an invisible (inner) wound. This is an example of what Taussig and Benjamin mean by corporeal knowing.

First Contact/Second Contact and Songhay Possession

Taussig's disquisition on mimesis and alterity also—and importantly—considers the interpersonal dynamics of mimicry, especially during colonial encounters. Combing the historical record, he demonstrates the central role of mimicry in various first contacts—first meetings between Europeans, like Charles Darwin on the *Beagle,* and primitive alters, like the early nineteenth-century Fuegians. The latter are seen as great mimics. European first observers, by contrast, thought themselves poor mimics, a talent reserved for naturalized primitives. The apperceived role of mimesis, as demonstrated by Taussig's analysis, played a central role in the personal dynamics of these historic first encounters.

It is however, the dynamics of what Taussig calls "second contact" that is of central concern here. In "second contact," a person sees himself or herself refracted in the images produced by alters. Taussig writes of the disarmingly ferocious shock of "second contact," which is often overtly political.

One of the most illustrious cases of second contact is that of Igbo Mbari houses of southeastern Nigeria, in which sculptures depicting colonial white men are erected in isolated forest shrines: images of pith-helmeted, bespectacled white men emerging from the ground, of African whitemen, wearing coats and ties, speaking into a microphone.[37]

Second contact, in fact, is a primary feature of spirit possession among the Songhay people of Niger and Mali. In the bodies of mediums many of the Songhay spirits become replicas of ancestors who embody the past, make contact with the present, and determine the future. The Genji Bi spirits, for example, embody the first occupiers of Songhay lands, the Kurumba and Gurmantche people who today live just to the west of the Songhay. The Genji Bi are spirits of soil fertility, beings who don clothing that exposes their legs and chests, who wash themselves with soil, and who sing rather than talk. These spirits are primitive alters to the civilized Songhay, who cover their legs and chests, who wash with water, and who sing only rarely. This Songhay reproduction of their neighbors' ancestors, the Genji Bi, is reminiscent of Darwin and Captain Fitzroy's naturalized, primitivist take on the Fuegians.

First contact between the conquering Songhay and conquered Kurumba and Gurmantche peoples occurred in the fifteenth century. From a dispossessed Kurumba-Gurmantche perspective, second contact occurs at every Gengi Bi possession ceremony, for they see themselves through the culturally stylized embodiment of spirit possession. This kind of second contact would be similar to literate Fuegians reading Charles Darwin or Captain Fitzroy or to an educated colonial Songhay reading about his primitiveness in a colonial report. Although this kind of second contact is usually from the vantage of the dispossessed, it is no less shocking than a white man seeing himself depicted in African or Cuna sculpture.

The same kind of dispossessed second contact occurs during

Doguwa spirit ceremonies. The Doguwa, spirits from the Hausa-speaking east of Niger, came into the Songhay pantheon early in the twentieth century, following a wave of Hausa migration into Songhay country. These spirits are mean, crass, mercurial; they drink blood, devour honey, and drive their victims insane before killing them. Among the Doguwa, men sometimes dress as women. Males and females use foul language and pay little attention to the filth that soils their bodies. Not a pretty portrait, and yet when these ceremonies are performed there are Hausa-speaking people in the audience who, like Taussig confronting the Cuna figurines, may experience the electroshock of second contact.

Second Contact: The Hauka

Second contact, then, is usually a two-way street. The spirits of the Songhay pantheon, including the Hauka, are the embodiment of the Songhay imagination, which, lest we forget, incorporates African as well as European universes of experience and affects African as well as European audiences—in very different ways.

"Second contact" is a shocking disruption to the neat and tidy categories of European conceptual hegemony. Taussig describes this disruption with eloquence.

To become aware of the West in the eyes and handiwork of its Others, to wonder at the fascination with their fascination, is to abandon border logistics and enter into the 'second contact' era of the borderland where "us" and "them" lose their polarity and swim in and out of focus. This dissolution reconstellates the play of nature in mythic pasts of contractual truths. Stable identity formations auto-destruct into silence, gasps of unaccountable pleasure, or cartwheeling confusion gathered in a crescendo of what I call "mimetic excess" spending itself in a riot of dialectical energy.[38]

For Taussig, the Hauka deities are a particularly compelling example of second contact, for they mimic colonial personages. Like any deities in spirit possession, Hauka mediums are and are not the Europeans they so frighteningly and comically depict. Taussig's second contact with the Hauka is through the "mechanical reproduction" of the film camera—Jean Rouch's aforementioned classic ethnographic film, *Les maîtres fous.* Taussig describes a magic moment in the film that, for him, encapsulates magical mimesis. It is a jump cut from the sacrifice of an egg on the statue of the governor (of the colonial Gold Coast) to the military parade that celebrates the opening of the Colonial Assembly in Accra. One is teleported from watching an egg run over the governor's statue—a copy, after all—to the real governor.

The film hurls us at the cascading yellow and white plumes of the white governor's gorgeous hat as he reviews the black troops passing. Those of us watching the film in a university lecture hall gasp. There is something immensely powerful released at this moment, begging for interpretation. The film with its ability to explore the optical unconscious, to come close and enlarge, to frame and to montage, creates in this sudden juxtaposition a suffusion of mimetic magic.[39]

Separated from the Hauka deities by screen and space, Taussig's analysis captures—for a Western audience—a magic moment of second contact; it is a telling example of the "Western rebirth of the mimetic faculty by means of modernity's mimetic machinery."[40]

For Songhay audiences as well as for the European occupying the body of an anthropologist, the terrifying antics of the Hauka, however, are something other than Taussig's narrowly defined "second contact." Their presence is a shock to everyone, but Songhay observers, I would guess, are not so much concerned with the rebirth of mimesis in Euroamerica; rather, they continuously express their worries about their precarious fate in the world.

What is it about the Hauka that compels a middle-aged Nigerien man with a doctorate in soil science to attend their ceremonies and keep in his house a "copy" of Commandant Bashiru's pith helmet? What is it about the Hauka that prompts the European occupying the body of an anthropologist to bear his Hauka burden? What is it about the Hauka that caused the military, which once controlled the Nigerien state, to use Hauka aesthetics as a model of political action?

*   *   *

The clang of cattle bells announces dusk in Tillaberi. The Haukas have come, settled their Roundtable business, and gone. No one leaves Adamu Jenitongo's compound, however, for one medium, the man who had been possessed by Bambara Mossi, is thrashing about in the sand. The musicians play Hauka rhythms. A deep groan rolls through the air as yet another Hauka arrives in the social world. He is Chefferi, "the non-believer."

Chefferi sweeps up from the sand and squats like a wrestler. He tears at his trousers, ripping them off just above the knee. He yanks off his shirt and wraps it around his head like a woman's head scarf. He pounds his chest, pushes through the circle of onlookers, and struts over to Adamu Jenitongo.

"Albora. Albora."

"Yes," says Adamu Jenitongo in response to the respectful term used for wise old men.

"Albora," he repeats. "You must make *kusu* [magic cake] for the other Anasaara here."

"That's fine," says Adamu Jenitongo.

"Tell your wife to bring me the finest millet seeds. And then bring me the biggest and heaviest mortar and pestle here."

Adamu Jenitongo asks his senior wife for these things.

Chefferi runs his finger through a small bowl filled with golden millet seeds. "These are good." He picks up the pestle. "Not big or heavy enough. Find me a proper pestle."

A young girl runs to the neighboring compound for a bigger pestle. Holding on to the dish, Chefferi bounds over to the canopy. "Play my music," he demands.

The musicians play Hauka rhythms. Dressed like a woman, Chefferi, big, black, thick, and frightening, stands at the center a large crowd. Night has fallen and the compound is illumined by the dim glow of kerosene lanterns that hang from the canopy's rafters. Like a circus performer, Chefferi waves at the crowd. "I, the Hauka non-believer, am going to give *kusu* to this Anasaara." He points at the anthropologist.

A young woman brings Chefferi two five-foot pestles carved from heavy hardwood. "These are good." He then lies on his back, and calls for two strong young women—millet pounders. One of the women puts the heavy mortar on Chefferi's bare chest. "Put the millet in the mortar," he orders, "and pound it until it becomes a fine white flour. The women do as they are instructed and begin to pound. The pestles thump the mortar with great force. The sound of the thumps are in counterpoint to Chefferi's moans of pain. The audience gapes at the wondrous spectacle.

The millet flour is soon as white and smooth as dune sand, and Chefferi triumphantly invites the audience to inspect the contents of the mortar. The young women lift the leaden mortar off his chest, and he leaps to an upright position. Chefferi grabs the anthropologist's arm roughly. "Anasaara. Anasaara. That," he says pointing at the millet flour, "is for you."

"I thank you, Chefferi."

"Today, we had a Roundtable on this dune," Chefferi announces. "We Hauka solved our problems with grace, with dignity. Now I, Chefferi, the non-believer, give you this *kusu*. You are now my brother. May this *kusu* help you to solve your problems, also with grace and dignity. May it move you forward on your path. May your words be heard by many people. Do not forget the Hauka, Anasaara. Do not forget us!"

The women scoop the flour out of the mortar and put it into a wooden bowl. "Adamu Jenitongo, come here," Chefferi commands.

Slowly, the old man walks over to Chefferi.

"Albora, tomorrow prepare for this Anasaara, who is now my brother, this *kusu*. Prepare it so he may walk his path with grace and dignity, so they he will never forget us, never lose respect for us."

"This, I shall do," says Adamu Jenitongo.

"Good," says Chefferi. "It is time to return to Malia, to the Red Sea." The musicians hear this cue and begin to play Hauka music. Chefferi flies through the air and lands on his back.

*   *   *

Lying unconscious on the dune, Chefferi's being is momentarily lost between the worlds, between the Red Sea and Tillaberi, between the colonial past and the postcolonial present, between his presence and that of his medium. So it is when Hauka spirits encounter themselves and others in the netherworld between possession and "conscious."

Chefferi is neither "European" nor African; he is neither man nor woman, Christian nor Muslim. His unclassifiable body rocks with personal and political power. The Hauka embody difference that makes for many differences. They have the power to sicken or heal, read the past or predict the future, endanger or protect villages. The Hauka's powerful presence—their horrific/comedic embodiment—has been a model of and for political resistance, a model of and for governance in postcolonial Niger.

On that white hot day in 1987 Chefferi placed a heavy burden on the European who "occupied" the body of an anthropologist. He offered his chest as a platform on which to pulverize millet. He ordered Adamu Jenitongo to transform millet flour into magical *kusu*. When I ate that *kusu* an embodied bond was sealed between the Hauka and me, a bond that demands that I write about them, as they would say, with remembrance and respect. This chapter, then, partially bears my embodied burden. I humbly offer it to the Hauka with brotherly deference.

4

"CONSCIOUS" AIN'T CONSCIOUSNESS

Entering the Museum of Sensory Absence

> The important thing is making generations. They can burn
> the papers but they can't burn conscious, Ursa. And that's
> what makes the evidence. And that's what makes the ver-
> dict.
>
> — Gayl Jones's character Great Gram in *Corregidora*

In Chapter 3 I alluded to Gayl Jones's novel *Corregidora*, a haunting tale about cultural memory and the "counter-memories"
of four generations of Afro-Brazilian and African American
women. Throughout the novel the protagonist's great-grandmother talks repeatedly about "conscious" and how the memories of "conscious" are deeper than the "official" historical texts
and records. "Conscious," which Great Gram considers "evidence," is sedimented in the bodies of the women, all of whom
are haunted by the hulking presence of the Portuguese sailor
Corregidora, who owned, abused, and abandoned them. Jones
describes how these memories extend well beyond the protagonist's great-grandmother. Indeed, the fury and sadness of memory infuse the protagonist's voice, especially when Ursa sings
the blues at Happy's Club:

Sometimes I wonder about their desire, you know, Grandmama's and
Great Gram's. Corregidora was theirs more than hers. Mama could
only know, but they could feel. They were with him. What did they
feel? You know how they talk about hate and desire. Two humps on
the same camel? Yes, hate and desire both riding them, that's what I
was going to say. "You carry more than his name, Ursa," Mama would
tell me. And I knew she had more than memories. Something behind
her eyes. A knowing, a feeling of her own. But she'd speak only their
life. What was their life, then? Only a life spoken to the sounds of my

breathing or a low-playing Victrola. . . . Still there was what they never spoke . . . what even they wouldn't tell me. How all but one of them had the same lover? Did they begrudge her that? Was that their resentment? There was something. . . . They squeezed Corregidora into me, and I sung back in return.[1]

For Gayl Jones, then, collective memories are evoked through the senses, from sentiments so elemental that they are beyond words, beyond the constraints of the text. When Ursa sings the blues, cultural memory possesses her.

What can Ursa teach us about body and memory? What can Ursa's singing the blues teach us about the dynamics of perception? My tentative answer, which is taken up in this chapter, is that the Ursas of the world remind us, first and foremost, that perception does, indeed, devolve not only from the visual surfaces of textual bodies, but also from the depths of sentient sounds and the contours of repulsion/desire evoked by tastes and smells. The Ursas of the world, long consigned to the margins of social and intellectual life—to the domain of repressed memory—set a standard against which we can attempt to judge the faithfulness, if not the relevance, of our often errant wanderings in the sensuous vacuum between the intelligible and the sensible. In this chapter, then, I read four diverse essays on the sensuous body to demonstrate how vision, body politics, sensory anesthesia, and embodied memories define and redefine memory in modernity.

The Eyes of the World Are Upon Us

Film theorists have long discussed the revolutionary potential of the cinema—of vision. In the early Soviet Union, as Susan Buck-Morss suggests in her 1994 essay, "The Cinema Screen as Prosthesis of Perception," the cinema was seen as the most important political-ideological tool of Lenin's revolution.[2] In France, surrealists, especially the early Artaud, also saw the cinema as revolutionary, but on a more philosophical than political plane. Theorists have also debated how the cinema altered perception. Much has been written on how audiences jumped in reaction to the screen arrival of a train in the Lumière brothers' first film, *L'arrive d'un train dans la gâre de Ciotat* (1895). Eisenstein believed that the filmmaker framed the perception of the audience.[3] Bazin and Mitry believed in a more phenomenologically interactive theory of cinematic perception. Still others have looked to the cinema to ponder the relationship between image and desire, feminism and semiotics, feminism and psychoanalysis, theory and fiction, and film image and language.[4] One of the most philosophically rigorous studies of film is that of Gilles Deleuze. In his two-volume work *Cinéma* (1986, 1989), he discusses, among other matters, the perceptual intricacies of cinematic movement: framing, montage, action images, time images, thought, and cinema.

Although Deleuze's cogitations on taxonomies of the cinematic image are intellectually breathtaking, they describe the unique sensuousness of the cinema abstractly. Left out of this analysis is the tactility Walter Benjamin brought to the analysis of visual perception.[5] In her essay, Susan Buck-Morss explores the space of visual sensuousness to assess the cinema screen philosophically and sensually as a prosthesis of perception. The essay is an exercise in sensuous scholarship that cuts beneath the surface of business-as-usual textual analysis to explore the sensuous relations among cinematic images, embodied responses, and cultural memory.

Buck-Morss begins, oddly enough, with Husserl's phenomenological reduction, his époché. Husserl's preoccupation, she writes, is "with the philosophical eye, his strenuous attempt to 'inspect' mental acts until their essences can be purely, intuitively 'seen' as absolute and non-contingent."[6] She briefly describes the philosophical rigor associated with Husserl's "apodetic" and "eidetic" reductions, perceptual moves that enable observers to "see" universal essences that constitute a given object. Although Husserl is often criticized for his putative mysticism,

it is not medieval mysticism that provides the most accessible route to Husserl's project. If we wish to have a vision of the pure object, this "self-given" "absolute datum," which is neither physical thing nor psychological fact but (—wondrous phrase! —) an "intentionally inexistant entity," we would do best to put down the text, leave the lecture, and go to the movies.[7]

Indeed, at the movies one sees the apodetically reduced object of cognition. "It is absolute data grasped in purely immanent seeing" in which we "directly inspect the unity of cognition and object." It is cognition that "sees itself."[8]

At first audiences were incapable of making the phenemonological reductions necessary to apprehend the cinematic image. For them, the cinema screen did not exist; they jumped at the sight of an oncoming train; they panicked at the sight of a smiling severed head. Buck-Morss argues that "it took a certain transformation of the senses" for people to apprehend the cinema screen. Indeed, she suggests that the "surface of the cinema screen functions as an artificial organ of cognition. The prosthetic organ of the cinema screen does not merely duplicate human cognitive perception, but changes its nature."[9] In other words, the cinema is able to project universal images that are synesthetic shocks to the senses. It is through the cinema that audiences become sensually aware of large collectivities: traffic in cities, street demonstrations, or, as in Eisenstein's films, the "masses" as the prime agents of change in significant historical events. Clearly, the apprehension of war and the mass appeal of violence devolve from the prosthetic intricacies of the cinema screen.[10]

It is by way of the cinema screen, Buck-Morss tells us, that we can recognize what the Ursas of the world know all too well: that cognition is physical. The Surrealists recognized the sensuous power of the cinema screen. Artaud and Desnos, among others, realized that human beings are lulled into accepting the reality of the images in films and dreams, that (following the terminology of Lacan and Williams) human beings "misrecognize" the illusion of the image.[11] As a result, the scenarios of Artaud and Desnos attempt to construct films that would deconstruct our fundamental relationship to the cinematic image. These experiments failed for the most part; their power paled in comparison to the sensuous power of the cinematic image. Indeed, cinematic images, manipulated through framing, close-ups, and montage, not only transform our senses but heighten them. "They expose the nerve endings to extreme stimulation of the most shocking physical sensations: violence and torture, the terrifying and catastrophic, the tantalizing and erotic."[12]

Buck-Morss's analysis begs the question of how filmmakers, especially ethnographic filmmakers, should compensate for the sensuous terror that the cinematic image can unleash. Many of

the films of Jean Rouch display a healthy respect for the sensuous power of the cinematic image. Like his Surrealist men-
tors, Rouch uses film to provoke his audience. By the same
token he is fully aware of the power of the mass appeal of
cinematic images. He therefore makes films in collaboration
with those whom he films. In the case of his classic, *Les maîtres fous* (1956), one of the most provocative ethnographic films
ever made, Rouch prudently limited distribution for fear of
racist interpretation. And no wonder. The film includes scenes
of spirit-possessed black Africans handling fire, frothing at the
mouth, drinking blood gushing from a freshly slaughtered dog,
and chomping on dog meat, all the while imitating Europeans.
These images overwhelmed the subtle philosophical themes
embedded within and between the frames of the film.[13] Are
other ethnographic filmmakers equally sensitive to the sensuous power of the cinematic image? The message Buck-Morss is
sending to image makers—scholarly or whatnot—is that they
must not forget their ethical and political responsibilities in
a world in which the intelligible power of the text has been
eclipsed by the sensible power of the image. Image makers have
the power to provoke the audience sensuously, triggering an
array of powerful cultural memories. Filmmakers also have the
capacity to lull audiences into a happy insouciance serving up
an imageric pablum that reinforces what Renato Rosaldo calls
"imperialist nostalgia." The widespread commercial success of
the *Millennium* series, replete with its primitivist images and
messages, underscores the wisdom of Buck-Morss's message.[14]

Swedish Bodies

Jonas Frykman, a Swedish sociologist, has written of how officials of the Swedish welfare state constructed a social body—an
ideal Swedish body—as the foundation of the state.[15] His 1994
essay, "On the Move: The Struggle for the Body in Sweden in
the 1930's," underscores Buck-Morss's point about the universal appeal of mass images. It is a potent demonstration of the
curiously modernistic link of hypersensitivity and anesthesia.
Frykman argues that the sensory revolution that reconfigured
the Swedish body also reconfigured the Swedish body politic—
into the much admired modern welfare state. Indeed, admiring

commentators have long suggested the relationship between healthy bodies and healthy body politics.

Frykman analyzes links among local practices, cultural identity, and national politics in Sweden. Following Foucault, he argues that power comes from below. The transformation of Sweden from a relatively backward agrarian nation into the model of the modern welfare state, he writes, stems from local social movements that embodied the themes of modernism. The political transformation, which dates to the 1930s, devolved in part from the Swedish penchant for exercise—gymnastics. "Swedish gymnastics was not just an athletics movement; it showed the experiences, dreams, and power structures that helped to modernize Sweden in the 1930s."[16]

In inter-war Sweden, the enthusiasm for the new—the credo of modernism—was expressed not only through gymnastics but through vegetarianism, nudism, and athleticism. The new sensuousness in Sweden corresponded to a new sexual openness, which was articulated in books and newspapers as well as in the cinema. This articulation expressed the mass appeal of personal conquest. If one could conquer her or his body, one could meet the future and master it.

Frykman deftly situates the transformation of the Swedish body in Swedish space. Swedes had to conquer their bodies outdoors, breathing in fresh air as they toned their muscles. The air of the city, of course, was not up to the standards set for bodily conquest; one had to repair to the countryside, to pristine lakes and unspoiled mountains. From one's experience in the country, one could learn about living, about perfecting individual practices. Life in the countryside was simple, uncluttered, clear, natural, rational. Indeed, the transformation of Swedish bodies was soon linked to the promotion of a worthy and reasonable life, which had its Swedish roots in cultural memories of Lutheran piety.[17]

Frykman goes on to describe how the Social Democrats tapped this local ferment for fitness to engineer the welfare state. The Swedish government of the 1930s created a program to organize the population's everyday life, while reconstituting the Swedish body. This experiment exacted a price, according to Frykman: ordinary citizens deferred to the wisdom of those who knew best. Although Frykman only hints at how the state constructed its imagery, there is little doubt that it exercised an incredibly powerful influence over individual will. And yet, the transformation of Sweden devolved not only from the corridors of power but "in everyday actions and the reorganization of the senses." Indeed, "the body's role in the process lies in the demonstration that the new age was not something which people primarily understood; it was something which they felt they were actively conquering, testing, mastering."[18] In Sweden the transformation of the senses dulled difference and promoted the reconfiguration of cultural memories—to the state sanctioned blueprint for social change.

Viewed from Buck-Morss's vantage, the transformation of the Swedish body and body politic seems like a very successful case of national anesthetization. This change, as Frykman demonstrates, came from below—at first. But the movement for change was soon co-opted by reform-minded middle class intellectuals, who, in effect, colonized the already transformed Swedish body. Reading Frykman one gets the impression of a nation of contented citizens who follow those who know best; the sense that Swedes had left behind the zesty subjectivities of Great Gram's "conscious" in favor of the bland objectivities of consciousness. Difference appears to be obliterated as Swedish subjects are incorporated into the objectivized body politic. The celebrated Swedish success, which has been critiqued by Ingmar Bergman among others, forces us to recognize the power of State and corporate image-making to objectify difference, to excise the discordant. Through sensuousness, the State—not to discount the corporation—is able to shape memory and reinforce dominance.

Electronic Anesthesia

Buck-Morss and Frykman argue that, when confronted by the cinema, the human nervous system is modified in a seemingly paradoxical way. "On the one hand there is an extreme heightening of the senses, a hypersensitivity of nervous stimulation. On the other, there is a dulling of sensation, a numbing of the nervous system that is tantamount to corporeal anesthetization."[19] Frkyman's essay gives us an example of how the state-aided reorganization of the senses in Sweden resulted in the objectification of individual corporeality and the anesthetization of the body politic by those "who knew best."

In a 1994 essay, "From Desert Storm to Rodney King via ex-Yugoslavia: On Cultural Anaesthesia," Alan Feldman extends the arguments of Buck-Morss and Frykman by describing how the State is able to manipulate visual images to erase that which might stimulate people to resist. Put another way, he demonstrates how the State can use the senses to dull its subjects into blithely accepting the unacceptable.[20]

Feldman defines cultural anesthesia as "the banishment of disconcerting, discordant and anarchic sensory presences and agents that undermine normalizing and often silent premises of everyday life."[21] This take on cultural anesthesia devolves from Theodor Adorno, who suggested that in late modernity the "quantitative and qualitative increase of objectification increases the social capacity to inflict pain on the Other—and I would add—to render the Other's pain inadmissible to public discourse and culture."[22]

Based on Adorno's insight, Feldman calls for a politically sensitive anthropology of the senses. Feldman also suggests that sensory capacities are not evenly distributed in complex societies with cross-cutting sectors of economic, racial, ethnic, gender, and cultural domination. Since the time of Plato and Aristotle the senses, which have long been specialized and stratified, have been used by the Republic to legitimate the authority of the few. But the exponential stratification and specialization of the senses in modernity becomes especially poignant when we consider the potency of cinematic and other visual images and the power of the media and the State to sanitize them. In this way the state contours memory—through the physiognomic manipulation of the body.

Cultural anesthesia is, in fact, a direct descendant of realism. In the nineteenth century, Feldman points out, realism presupposed an omniscient observer who visualized reality through his narrations. In such a space, time becomes linear, regular, homogenized, and the subject becomes just one more aspect of representation—the obliteration of difference.[23] These cornerstones of scientific objectification become in the twentieth century part and parcel of burgeoning commodification, all of which transfers the discussion of the real from philosophical salons to consumer airwaves—radio, cinema, television, video. Such a transfer renders dear the power of the image, the symbol, the trademark.[24] Through the sanitization of the consumer image, bodies are depersonalized; they are one among any number of realist objects, all devoid of odors, distinction, and pain. This conceit, which devolves from Cartesianism, is also central to ongoing disembodied approaches to the human sciences.

Feldman sensuously describes a stew of images that has no flavor, no odor, no texture—only a tasteless, depersonalized surface image. These images put us to sleep, make us listless, make us impervious to that which "doesn't fit" within the stylized scope of things. Such a stew of images, according to Feldman, disembodies the subject. He powerfully demonstrates this process of symbolic evisceration through descriptions of the air-brushed media coverage of Operation Desert Storm and the imageric disembodiment of Rodney King.

In Operation Desert Storm, "The eulogized smartbombs were prosthetic devices," writes Feldman, "that extended our participant observation in the video occlusion of absented Iraqi bodies. Their broadcast images functioned as electronic simulacra that were injected into the collective nervous system of the audience as antibodies that inured the viewer from realizing the human-material consequence of the war."[25] Viewed from afar, the war became an entertaining light show that highlighted the technological wonders of the military. "We" were cashing in on the multi-billion dollar military investments of the Reagan years. Violence, death, and misery, however, did not seep through the visual images. After all, as Ursa's Great Gram would say, those "negatives" had become part of the "conscious" rather than the consciousness of war.

Feldman's analysis of the Rodney King debacle demonstrates what happens when "conscious" slips into consciousness, violating the carefully constructed realism of commodified facticity. Initially, the images of Los Angeles police mercilessly beating a defenseless King shocked people in the United States. These were graphic images of State-sponsored violence or making pain in Feldman's terms. No sanitized violence here. Initially, the image of King's brutal beating made him a subject-in-pain.

But "conscious," as Ursa's Great Gram knew so well, is exceedingly dangerous, even seditious; it must be transformed into consciousness. And so the invisible image-makers set about to totally objectify the pain-suffering subject.

The first step in objectification was to bestialize Rodney King. As Feldman points out, King was referred to as "bear-like," a being on his "haunches." Such objectification, to return to Adorno's point, augments the State's capacity to inflect pain. King is likened to an animal, symbolism that is consistent with longstanding racist imagery, the history of which can be traced to Herodotus through Gobineau to the present.[26] Incapable of language, the animal is silenced. Animals, moreover, do not feel pain. It is only "reasonable" for the police, who represent the State, to beat savage animals. To make matters worse, the police testified that King—or so they thought—was on PCP. And so the objectification of King—the sanitization of the violence brought upon his body—proceeds through frames of blackness, bestiality, narcosis, and finally, anesthesia.

"Conscious" in Feldman's language is "sensory alterity." He suggests that it is a high priority for social scientists to salvage "conscious" so as to compete with what he calls the realisms of the cinema and the law. Feldman's plea doesn't mean that anthropologists should naively "give voice" to the other. The role of the committed, sensuous scholar, rather, is to locate "lost biographies, memories, words, pains and faces which cohere into a vast secret museum of historical absence."[27] That is precisely the burden Great Gram delivers to Ursa. When Great Gram says that "they can burn papers but they can't burn conscious," she passes on to Ursa the burden of cultural memory. Ursa's burden is also that of contemporary anthropologists, who must increasingly monitor the anesthetizing ethers that the State continuously pulses into air.

Memories of the Senses

Feldman's analysis of cinematic and legal realism compels us to wonder where to find a sensuous "conscious" amid the evermore intricate netting of carefully constructed cultural camouflage. Feldman writes of lost biographies, words, gazes, and pains—an encyclopedia of "conscious." He also writes of a lecture given by an embattled Croatian folklorist. Although this woman spoke of reflexive anthropology, there was something in her talk that seeped through the rarefied discourse of texts, heteroglossia, and ethnographic authority. Her presentation was "a palpable and gendered self-reflexivity that had been channeled by the sensory remembrance of scheduled terror."[28] This folklorist was unable to erase the grief from her voice, unable to untangle the knots of pain from her body. Unable to deal with pain and grief, the audience intellectualized the discussion. Confronted by the alien primitive, the audience in Sweden transformed the fragmented chaos of the sensible into the holistic order of the intelligible. In the academy, as I've already suggested, only a small number of savants want to deal with the sensuous, with the "thrownness" of the emotions.

The alienation of grief, pain, and other emotions has a long history dating—in print at least—to Plato's *Republic*. Plato, of course, recommended the banishment of poets and dramatists from his Republic. Pandering to the heart's emotions, he reasoned, would upset the head's thoughts. And yet poetry is the elemental language, the expression par excellence of the human imagination. It is a cache of sensory alterity, of "conscious." It is one door into what Feldman calls "the secret museum of historical absence."[29]

In the previously discussed essays of Buck-Morss, Frykman, and Feldman the authors use the language of the academy to rethink the configuration of the senses in modernity. They present arguments that use the logic of the academy to subvert categories and assumptions. C. Nadia Seremetakis (1994) writes a text that both analyzes and evokes sensuousness. Her essay, "Memory of the Senses, Part II: Still Acts," employs the poetics of textual montage to fuse ethnographic description, cultural memory, and the conceptual problematics of modernity.[30] It is an artful essay that powerfully articulates the scholarly benefits of adopting a more poetically sensuous approach to the human sciences.

Seremetakis structures her article as a play in six acts: saliva, traffic, the journey, dust, from parlor to field, and reflexive commensality. Like a good play, each act is but a fragment of a whole—ethnography—that is itself riven with faults and fissures. She writes that "the use of montage here is not simply an aesthetic or arbitrary choice. Sensory and experiential fragmentation is the form in which this sensory history has been stored and this dictates the form of its reconstruction."[31]

Seremetakis tells the story of the Greek grandmother who feeds the Greek baby by chewing bread until it becomes a paste. She then takes the bread from her mouth and puts it into the baby's mouth. In this way bread and saliva bind grandmother and baby. In fact, metaphors of baking pervade Greek notions of socialization. "A woman raises a child as she raises dough into bread. Working the bread with the tongue and saliva, the grandma changes it to dough which is then used to raise the child."[32] In other words, to bake is to be enculturated. By the same token, social memory in Greece is baked/sung/smelled. Here Seremetakis underscores a fundamental flaw of the aforementioned body-as-text metaphor. In Seremetakis's essay the body is not only "read" and "written," it is also felt.

The memory of the senses, however, is never static. When one takes a trip in Greece, as described by Seremetakis, one's body, like that of the Songhay sorcerer or griot, is consumed by the world, by smells, by cultural memory.

Each smell generates its own textures and surfaces. No smell is encountered alone. There are combinations of smells that make up a unified presence: the grandma's house; the garden aroma combined with the animal dung; the oregano bunch hanging over the sheep skin containing the year's cheese; the blankets stored in the cabinet which combine rough wool with the humidity of the ocean; the oven exuding the smell of baking bread and the residue of ashes; the fresh bread in the open covered with white cotton towels.[33]

Such a range of smells, the strongest catalysts of memory, cannot be silenced. One can taste the various points on the journey from city to country. One can taste the seasons. Such descriptions cut to the heart of embodiment, a concept that many scholars understand only partially. Serematakis's essay teaches us a key lesson of the sensuous scholarship that I advocate in this book: that embodiment is not primarily textual, that the human body is not principally a text; rather, it is consumed by a world filled with smells, textures, sights, sounds, and tastes, all of which spark cultural memories.

The sights, sounds, smells, and tastes of Sermetakis's essay create a sensuous context for her ruminations on "reflexive commensality." "Between grandmas and grandchild sensory acculturation and the materialization of historical consciousness occurred through the sharing of food, saliva, and body parts."[34] For Seremetakis, this sharing produces a setting of commensality which she defines as "the exchange of sensory memories and emotions, and of substances and objects incarnating remembrance and feeling."[35] This path is one that leads us to the secret museum that Feldman evokes: the museum of sensory absence.

Of Dust and Anthropology

For much of its history, anthropology has been a dusty discipline. History, of course, is renowned as *the* dusty discipline—all those years that historians spend amid the archival dust. Although increasing numbers of historically-minded anthropologists have experienced archival dust, the dustiness of anthropology is qualitatively different. In anthropology, dust reflects age, a condition which, in turn, valorizes authenticity. There is also in anthropology the ultimately unattainable quest for the culturally pristine—so artfully and painfully described in Lévi-Strauss's *Tristes tropiques.* Unable to obtain the unobtainable, anthropologists perfected the practice of "dusting off." Archaeologists have "dusted off" bones and pots to "expose" a "culture complex." Based on "data" collected during fieldwork, cultural anthropologists have "dusted off" social structures, kinship systems, exchange systems, cognitive maps, symbolic inversions, domestic modes of production, transnational networks, and even postcolonial ethnoscapes.

When the anthropologist first enters the field site the sensory organization of modernity, the perceptual history and commensal structure of the discipline direct him/her to first see dust. Without long-term fieldwork and sensory archaeology the anthropologist may never come to know that this dust is a surface residue of the researcher's own acculturation that obscures depth: other sensory surfaces that embody alternative materialities, commensualities and histories. Without a reflexive anthropology of the senses, fieldwork, short or long, remains trapped in the literal, captive of realist conventions that are themselves unacknowledged historically determined perceptual and commensal patterns. This is well understood by those who inhabit the memory of other sensory and material reciprocities. How can they take anthropologists seriously when the latter go with the dust?[36]

Unreflexive dusting off, as Seremetakis would agree, not only cleans an object of so much sedimentation, but also kicks up clouds that obscure one's vision. Dusting off is part and parcel of a methodology that builds what Seremetakis, Feldman, and Buck-Morss would call sensory anesthesia. The images of cinema and the airwaves, as has been suggested in this chapter, can create veritable dust storms that irritate our eyes, narrow our nasal passages, clog our pores, swell our tongues, and infect our ears. These storms engulf us in clouds of dust that cut us off from embodied memories of pain, terror, love, loss, poetry, sensibility, grandmas and Great Grams, from memories of the secret history hidden in the museum of sensory absence.

In the past social scientists have, indeed, usually gone with the dust. In the future perhaps we shall become "conscious" of a wind that blows in more than one direction.

PART 3
EMBODIED REPRESENTATIONS

Introduction: Embodying the Grammar

> Someone divides mankind into buyers and sellers and forgets that buyers are sellers too. If I remind one of this is his grammar changed?
>
> —Wittgenstein

It has long been a curious habit in the academy to divide the world into buyers and sellers. This absolutist tendency has created all sorts of cross-cutting distinctions that reinforce the illusion of a classically ordered universe. Realists distinguish themselves from idealists and vice versa. Hard scientists distinguish themselves from soft humanists and vice versa. And if someone, like Wittgenstein, reminds the realists and scientists that they are also idealists and humanists, is that enough to alter their grammar?

Usually not, for academic grammars tend to be rather entrenched, so entrenched, in fact, that the goal of many scholars—scientists and humanists alike—is to aspire to competence practiced with a dead hand. All of which leads to a fine-tuned intellectual stagnation. And yet, as Kirsten Hastrup has noted: "The desire for fixed standards in science is challenged by the frightening indeterminacy of experience."[1] A few scholars have suggested that a re-invigorated Romanticism might be one solution to a stagnant academicism. Richard Shweder has argued that the project of Romanticism has been "to dignify subjective experience, not to deny reality; to appreciate imagination, not to disregard reason; to honor our differences, not to underestimate our common humanity."[2] Given this approach to the human sciences "there are no facts without value, no reason without emotion, and no knowledge without experience."[3]

In this book I am attempting to move one step beyond Shweder's reconstituted Romanticism into a fully sensuous scholarship in which experience and reality, imagination and reason, difference and commonality are fused and celebrated in both rigorous and imaginative practices as well as in expository and evocative expression. So far, we have seen how ever-changing local epistemologies affect the search for understanding and the production of knowledge. We have also seen how the body is more than a surface for social inscription: it is a repository of "conscious," of existential memory that fleshes out that which has been forgotten or erased from the past. In this final section of *Sensuous Scholarship*, the chapters have been shaped to demonstrate the kind of flexible representation that underscores the linkages of experience and reality, imagination and reason, difference and commonality. In Chapter 5, "Spaces, Places, and Fields," West African street vendors construct a local epistemology in the hybrid spaces of New York City. The chapter describes the sensuous circumstances of the vendors, but also includes an analysis of cross-cultural conflicts in local politics as well as a theoretical rumination on how cultural hybridity challenges the very foundation of the human sciences. In Chapter 6, "Artaud, Rouch, and the Cinema of Cruelty," I craft an analysis of the philosophical foundations that structured the work of two of this century's most notable image-makers, Antonin Artaud and Jean Rouch—sensuous scholars both.

The chapters in Part Three point to the desirability of the epistemological flexibility of an embodied grammar. Flexibility of approach is not at all a call for a naive epistemological relativism, but rather an argument for imagination and creativity as well as rigor and mastery.

5
SPACES, PLACES, AND FIELDS

The Politics of West African Trading in New York City's Informal Economy

The "field" in anthropology is becoming a dizzying array of cross-cutting transnational spaces that take place in zones of multiple contestation. Consider the kaleidoscopic forces that converged in mid-October 1994, on New York City's 125th Street, the cultural crossroads of Harlem. The 125th Street Vendors Association, a loosely organized "union" of some 500 African American vendors and West African traders from Senegal, Mali, Niger, and The Gambia, threaten to shut down 125th Street if Mayor Giuliani makes good on his campaign promise to disperse the African market from Harlem's main thoroughfare. Although the "union" is supported by the Nation of Islam whose ministers preach versions of Islamic purity and African American self-sufficiency, some members of the "union" dislike and distrust Nation of Islam leader Louis Farrakhan. Many of the West African traders wonder how and why such a man calls himself a Muslim. The vendors are also supported by the Reverend Al Sharpton, who uses his particular orientation to Christianity to articulate his solidarity with hard-working African and African American people. After the market's dispersal, Sharpton gets arrested for peddling Bibles on 125th Street. There are also supportive Asian and African American shop owners on 125th Street who think that the crowds brought in by the African market are good for business. There are, of course, just as many Asian and African American shop owners who think the presence of the vendors is bad for business. They say that the vendors are disrespectful and dirty and engage in unfair business practices.

Like the Nation of Islam, the Masjid Malcolm Shabazz promotes Islamic austerity and African American self-sufficiency.
The religious organization that follows the path of its founder,
Malcolm X, promotes a plan to regulate the vendors, suggesting that the unregulated 125th Street market be moved nine
blocks south of the shopping district to the Masjid Malcolm
Shabazz International Plaza, their regulated and city-sanctioned
site at 116th Street and Lenox Avenue, a commercially depressed space. They want to charge the vendors a registration
fee, which would make them "legal," as well as daily rent. In exchange, they would monitor the market's cleanliness and security. This idea is endorsed by the Harlem Business Alliance and
the Harlem Urban Development Corporation. Both organiza-
tions promote economic ties to West Africa, but do not like the
cluttered, unregulated presence of an open-air African market
on Harlem's major business boulevard. Such a presence may
well be intolerable, for it suggests spatially that Harlem's economic renaissance is but an illusion. Harlem's elected officials
who have vested interests in economic development also support the 125th Street crackdown and the Masjid's "generous
offer." The Masjid's plan is also welcomed warmly by the Giuliani administration. And why not! The plan co-opts a generally
revered African American religious institution and provides a
peaceful alternative to violent racial confrontation—something
no mayor would want. At the same time, City Hall would receive 30 percent of the revenues that the Masjid collects, meaning that it would collect taxes from previously unlicensed and
non-taxpaying vendors. In exchange City Hall would police the
market and clean the streets regularly. The plan also provides
positive political payoffs for the Giuliani Administration. Giuliani could say that he is keeping his political promises. Police
Commissioner Bratton could say he is following through on his
promise to enforce city regulations which, as we shall see, are
at odds with the practices of an informal economy.

Most of the West African traders, who say that their presence reinvigorated the economy of 125th Street, are seemingly
powerless pawns in the game of New York City's political and
cultural discourse. And yet they, like the exceedingly diverse
African American community in Harlem, weave crazy quilts of
their own. The Senegalese, for example, have been in New York

City since 1982 and are well represented among the West African traders in Harlem. Some Senegalese, most notably people well established in various businesses, support the market move to 116th Street. Many Senegalese street vendors, however, oppose the mayor's crackdown. These differences are exacerbated by ethnic, regional, and religious differences. Senegalese from the Casamance, the south, are less likely to be tied into economic and religious networks that are controlled by majority peoples (Wolof, Serere) from the north. Many of the Senegalese in New York City, moreover, are also devotees of the Mourid Sufi order, which, according to Malien and Nigerien street vendors, has invested capital in the Masjid Malcolm Shabazz, giving the Masjid's market plan a putative behind-the-scenes Senegalese connection. Vendors from Mali react to the market's dispersal with pragmatic resignation. Although they all want to remain at the African market, they refuse to march with the 125th Street Vendors Association on October 17. Some of them decide to pay $100 to register at the Masjid 116th Street market; others, who blame the African market's demise on the Senegalese, refuse to pay money to people who want to ruin their trading businesses. Several recently arrived people from Niger march in the vendors' October 17th demonstration. Most of the more established Nigerien traders, however, do not participate, even though they too want to remain on 125th Street. Thinking that the cost of trading on Canal Street, where it costs as much as $2500 a month to rent store front shelf space, would be too expensive, some of them agree to move their operations to 116th Street; others refuse to do so. The Nigeriens angrily blame the market's demise on the greed of the African American community, for which they have little respect and much distrust.

In the remainder of this chapter I attempt to analyze the social, political, and cultural forces that led to the market's demise. I first evoke sensuously the spatial dynamics of the African market in Harlem. Incorporating the dimension of power to the analysis of space, I present the recent convoluted history of contested vending spaces in New York City. It is a history of conflicting spatial practices and volatile cultural politics, rendered even more complex by Police Commissioner William Bratton's "bottom-up" philosophy of policing cities. I then detail how and why the police "cleaned up" 125th Street and how

African American and West African vendors reacted to the mayoral crackdown. The chapter concludes with a discussion of the significance of transnational public spaces for future anthropologies.

Market Space in Harlem

New York City, October 15, 1994. Two bowtied and black suited men hawk Nation of Islam pamphlets and sell bean pies on the northeast corner of 125th Street and Lenox Avenue, the commercial crossroads of Harlem. People stream along the sidewalks. The intersection is choked with traffic: buses transporting people to appointments uptown and downtown, fleets of large delivery trucks on their rounds, late model cars blaring rap music as they pass through, and older and more silent clunkers with hand-printed signs that say "livery" or "taxi." These gas guzzlers are gypsy cabs, the main substitute for taxis in the poorer neighborhoods of New York City; their drivers discharge and pick up fares at 125th and Lenox. The crowds thicken considerably, however, on the west side of Lenox Avenue at 125th Street, the site of the African market. From a distance, the market is a collage of parked vans, aluminum tables, incense smoke, and brilliantly colored imported print cloth. People saunter through this space, pausing here to chat, there to bargain and perhaps buy Ghanaian kente cloth, Kenyan baskets, Nigerien leather bags, Meccan incense, West African trade beads, or Tuareg silver jewelry. They might also select from assortments of "trademarked" American T-shirts, sunglasses, handbags, and baseball caps, almost all of which are manufactured in export processing zones outside the United States.

At first glance the African market appears a mass of disorganization. Sidewalks are seemingly cluttered with vendors' tables. To an outsider, chaos seems to govern where or what a vendor might sell. But first impressions are usually misleading, for the space of the African market is indeed organized albeit informally.

Such informal organization is the hallmark of markets throughout West Africa. Like the market in Harlem, the movement of goods and people through open market space in West Africa also appears chaotic to outsiders—at least initially. It is

Figure 7. African art displayed on West 53rd Street several paces from the Museum of Modern Art in Manhattan, summer 1996. Photo: Jasmin Tahmaseb McConatha.

well known, however, that the space of most West African markets is often if not always apportioned and regulated through informal mechanisms.[1] In those markets members of the same ethnic groups or small villages cluster and sell the same kind of merchandise. In the larger Songhay/Zarma markets in the Republic of Niger, for example, Fulani herders sell cattle, milk, and butter; Hausa people butcher and sell meat; Yorubas from Nigeria sell pots, pans, and hardware; Songhay/Zarma people sell grain and spices—all from informally designated spaces. The story of markets in West Africa entails much sociological and religious complexity. The lure of trade and markets spurred the medieval spread of Islam from North to West Africa.[2] The attraction of centralized urban markets also sparked much urban migration throughout West African history.[3] The more than one-hundred-year history of migration—long and short term—of Songhay and Hausa from Niger to the Guinea Coast is a case in point.[4] In the political arena, Islam provided the context for the construction of specific religious identities (Qadiriyya, Tijaniyya, Muridiyya, Hammalliya, Wahhabiyya) that have continuously fragmented local, regional, and state social relations in West Africa.[5] No matter the extent of frictions generated by this religious fragmentation, it has not usually interfered with trade. As Emmanuel Grégoire wrote in his study of Islam and identity among Hausas in Niger, "A marabout explained, 'You can do business with anybody; what's important is to earn a profit.' Another went even further: 'Money has no smell, and you can, indeed, do business with non-Muslims, with Christians for example.'"[6]

This rich and complex set of traditions and practices influences the attitudes and behaviors of West African traders at the African market in Harlem. In terms of the spatial allocation of market tables, the 125th Street space is organized like many West African markets, though more through country of origin than through ethnic identity. Malians, for example, are the principal cloth merchants. They sell from tables and stalls along both sides of the wide Lenox Avenue sidewalk. Pockets of Malians can also be found along the north sidewalk of 125th Street. Senegalese and Gambians occupy the northwestern corner of 125th and Lenox, where they sell trade beads, incense, leather bracelets decorated with cowrie shells, earrings, and rings, also decorated with cowrie shells. Farther west on 125th Street, one passes some African Americans selling religious books, including the Qur'an. One bookseller hawks Afrocentric titles as well as cassettes. He displays the books on two tables; the videos, including lectures by Ivan Van Sertima, are projected on a television set on the roof of the vendor's parked car—a complex articulation of multiple ideologies in the space of fifty feet.

Farther west on the north side of 125th Street, one approaches the Carver State Bank as well as vendor space taken by men from Niger. Some of these vendors sell handbags from

Korea; others hawk straw hats from China or straw bags from Kenya. One man offers woven bags from Turkey and leather bags from Niger. Another sells sunglasses from Chinatown in the summer and pirated videos in the winter. In order to test the quality of the videos he has a television and video playback machine all wired to a car battery underneath his vending table.[7] Other Nigeriens sell baseball caps with the insignia of professional and college sports teams. Other caps, T-shirts, and sweat shirts are inscribed with trademarked social messages from Spike Lee or trademarked names like Hugo Boss, Karl Kani, or Timberland. Into this cultural kaleidoscope, West African street merchants bring trading traditions that are profoundly shaped by Islam. Indeed, money has no smell on the sidewalks of Harlem, and these merchants have no regrets about selling copies of the latest "ethnic" chic. As one trader admitted, "we will sell anything to anyone, even drug dealers who have lots of cash. We don't believe in drugs or drug dealing, but we are in business, are we not?"[8]

Moving westward, one approaches the Adam Clayton Powell State Office Building. Here there are Senegalese selling sunglasses, including Ray Bans, dolls, and jewelry. A vendor from Uganda sells print reproductions of batiks. Toward the corner of 125th Street and Seventh Avenue, Jamaicans sell what the West African vendors call "wood," statues carved in Africa.[9] Much of this "wood" is carved in the image of West African colonial officials, the ubiquitous "colon," a type of African art that has become economically viable. These dreadlocked men from the Caribbean, situated among closely-cropped West Africans, sell "authentic" images of Africa to African American shoppers whose urge to buy "wood" is compelled by longstanding notions of African pride, most of which are incomprehensible to the Africans "represented" by the statuettes. Ironically, such incomprehensibility charges the market with energy.

Unlike West African markets, none of these "national" spaces in Harlem are purely "national."[10] A few African American vendors can be found among the Maliens, Senegalese, and Nigeriens. Several Maliens sell from tables among the Nigeriens. Small clusters of Senegalese sit next to Jamaicans. No "national" space is inviolable at the African market.

Such informality gives this open-air market space an easy,

festive air. Double-decker buses from Apple Tours bring camera packing Europeans to "shoot" the African market—from a safe distance. Swarms of shoppers freely move up and down the sidewalks looking at bags, touching print fabrics, trying on straw hats or jewelry. Their movement through space is constrained only by the presence of other shoppers and by Senegalese women selling African food from shopping carts.

The vendors talk freely to shoppers in variously sophisticated forms of an American English influenced by local African American idioms. Prices are fairly rigid for baseball caps, scarves, and gloves. They are less so for African merchandise, for which many shoppers bargain. Refusing to bargain or buy, some of the shoppers complain about high prices.[11]

The traders converse among themselves in English, French, and a variety of West African languages, enjoying the banter that comes with periodic lulls in trading. During their afternoon prayers, the vendors look after one another's merchandise—informal protection against the ever-present threat of theft.

Although the vendors at the African market occasionally violate any number of minor city regulations and trademark and copyright statutes, the police seem subdued. Their primary preoccupation, it seems, is to enforce parking regulations, especially along 125th Street. Otherwise they tend to leave the vendors alone.

The easy, festive openness of the African market, however, came to an abrupt end on October 17, 1994, when Mayor Giuliani ordered it closed.

A Brief History of the African Market

Although African Americans have a long history of vending on the streets of Harlem, the first West African vendors did not migrate uptown until 1990.[12] A Senegalese art dealer claims to be the first African to vend on 125th Street.[13] He was soon joined by other Senegalese, Maliens, and Nigeriens. Gradually, the African character of the 125th Street market became more and more dominant.

Prior to 1990 the primary practitioners of informal street trading in New York City were Senegalese men vending from tables set up along mid-town Manhattan sidewalks. Given the regulatory difficulties of obtaining a vending license in New York City, the majority of the Senegalese conducted unlicensed operations.[14] By 1985 scores of Senegalese had set up tables in front of some of Manhattan's most expensive retail space on Fifth Avenue. Such a cluttered informal Third World place in a First World space soon proved intolerable to the Fifth Avenue Merchants Association. Headed by Donald Trump, the Association urged the City Hall to crack down on unlicensed vendors.

Following the "clean-up," Senegalese vendors relocated to less precious spaces in Midtown: Lexington Avenue, 42nd Street near Grand Central Station, and 34th Street near Times Square, to name several of the locations. They also worked in teams to protect themselves from the authorities and petty criminals. One person would sell goods at his table. His compatriot partners would post themselves on corners as lookouts. Another compatriot would serve as the bank, holding money safely away from the trade. In this way, Midtown side streets became Senegalese turf. As more and more Senegalese arrived in New York City, the vending territory expanded north to 86th Street on the East Side and south to 14th Street in Greenwich Village and Canal Street in Lower Manhattan. In some areas the Senegalese replaced vending tables with attache cases filled with "Rolex" and other "highend" watches. The vendor would stand on a Midtown corner with his attache case open for casual inspection. A man with an attache case—even an open one—in Midtown blends in with First World spatial surroundings. Besides, he had his lookouts across the street and his money holder at mid-block. This strategy made these vendors more mobile and less visible. It also demonstrates how the Senegalese confounded mainstream American spatial assumptions to their own economic advantage.

By 1990 the Senegalese had a lockhold on informal vending space in most of Manhattan. Backed by the considerable financial power of the Mourids, the Muslim Sufi brotherhood in Senegal to which the vast majority of Senegalese vendors belonged, the Senegalese soon became the aristocracy of African merchants in New York.[15] When merchants from Mali and Niger immigrated to New York City in 1990, the Senegalese had already saturated the lucrative Midtown markets, compelling them to set up their tables along 125th Street in Harlem. As West African vendors trickled into Harlem between 1990 and 1992, the African market grew, extending west from the corners of 125th Street and Lenox Avenue to 125th Street and Adam Clayton Powell Boulevard. Although vendors reported that business was only fair during the week, on weekends the market swelled with shoppers. By 1992 the African market had become one of New York City's tourist attractions. "Before we brought African things here," said one Nigerien vendor, "125th was deserted. No one came here. People were afraid of little bandits and drugs. When we came here we brought crowds and tourists. We revitalized 125th Street."[16]

The growth and success of the market brought with it a bevy of political problems in New York City. Like the Fifth Avenue Merchants Association, the Harlem Business Alliance lobbied the Dinkins administration to disperse the "illegal" vendors. With the support of Harlem's elected officials (federal, state, and city), the Dinkins administration decided, albeit reluctantly, to enforce the city's vending ordinances. The enforcement plan proved to be a dismal failure. In protest against the decision, the 125th Street Vendors Association, comprised of African American and West African street merchants, staged a demonstration that shut down 125th Street for a day. Although the police voiced their willingness to disperse the protestors, Dinkins, fearing the violent consequences of a police-vendor confrontation, backed down.

The market continued to grow following Dinkins's capitulation. In March 1993, vendors reported hearing rumors about the imminent dispersal of the market. "We hear these things all the time," one merchant said. "But we are not worried. Last time they tried to shut us down, we shut down all of 125th Street. They will leave us alone."[17] Most of the vendors I talked to seemed more worried about the effect of cold weather on sales than on City Hall's regulatory enforcement. Rumors nonetheless persisted throughout the spring and into the summer of 1993.

On August 19, 1993 bureaucrats from the New York City Department of Business Services distributed the following letter to the vendors on 125th Street.

Dear Vendor:

The New York City Department of Business Services with assistance from the 125th Street Local Development Corporation, the Harlem Business Alliance, Community Board #10, the 125th Street Vendors Association, and members of the business and street vendor communities have been working together to improve business conditions on 125th Street.

You should be aware that the law currently prohibits almost every form of street vending that now exists on 125th Street. This is why we are now proposing to establish an open air market for street vendors on 126th Street between Adam Clayton Powell Blvd. and St. Nicholas Avenue as a way to provide an alternative legal site for vendors. We will also work with the vendors currently at Malcolm X Blvd from 125th to 126th Streets on a plan to legally remain at this site. This solution is being presented to you as a way to provide a legitimate place for you to conduct your business.

In order for you to participate in this program, you should fill out the vendor registration form and mail it to the New York City Department of Business Services, 110 William Street, New York, New York. 10038, Attention: Intragovernmental Business Affairs Division. This information will be used for vendor identification cards, to determine the exact location of street vendor spaces and other requirements for the street vendor market.

We appreciate your cooperation and assistance to make the 126th Street alternative site a success. Thank you for your time and attention.[18]

The form requested the following information: name, address, telephone number, the nature of goods sold, and the number of tables used for vending. Many vendors provided the requested information; some furnished false names, addresses, and phone numbers; others simply refused to comply with the request for information.

In the end it didn't matter whether the vendors complied with the Department of Business Services request, for City Hall solved the problem of unlicensed vending on 125th Street the usual way—by doing nothing substantive. City Hall held meetings with the concerned parties: the Harlem Urban Development Corporation, the Harlem Business Alliance, and the 125th Street Vendors Association. People vented their frustrations and City Hall scheduled additional meetings; more vented frustrations, more meetings. Meanwhile, the African market continued to grow. Despite these ongoing negotiations all parties knew that nothing would be resolved until after the mayoral election in November 1993. "When Dinkins was a teenager," one vendor told us, "he peddled on the streets on Harlem. He will not deny us our living."[19]

Closing Spaces

In November 1993, Mayor Dinkins lost his reelection bid to Rudolph Giuliani, the Reagan-appointed former U.S. attorney for New York City. One strong reason for Giuliani's victory was his pledge to make New York more "liveable," by which he meant crime-free. Considering this seemingly insurmountable pledge, Giuliani's choice of William J. Bratton as Police Commissioner became his most important and politically significant appointment. Prior to his appointment, Bratton had secured his reputation by successfully policing Boston. In concert with Giuliani's views, Bratton believed in consistent and energetic enforcement of regulations. This belief meant that one begins to police a city from the bottom up—through the enforcement of penalties against minor regulatory infractions that sometimes cause minor headaches for citizens. Such enforcement, according to Bratton's theory, compels people to believe that there is some semblance of law and order in the streets. In this way one begins to order the perception of chaotic urban clutter and make the city more liveable.

Soon after his appointment, Bratton presented to the press a detailed outline of his pragmatic philosophy of law enforcement. He spoke about the presence of "Squeegee men" in Manhattan. These men, mostly unemployed African-Americans unlicensed by City Hall, approach motorists stuck in Manhattan traffic and propose to wash their windshields for a modest fee. In some instances they wash windshields without the consent of motorists and aggressively demand money. Although such unregulated activity hardly constitutes a major law enforcement problem, it constitutes a nuisance in Commissioner Bratton's universe of meaning. By eradicating the nuisance, following Bratton's logic, one takes a small but significant step toward making New York City a better place to live—at least for those who commute into Manhattan.[20]

Commissioner Bratton's proclamation can be read as a declaration of war against the informal economy of New York City in which the exchange of goods and services are unregulated by the state.[21] Participants in informal economies, which have grown exponentially since 1980, would include

the parent who purchases day care service without filling out social security forms, the unlicensed gypsy cab driver who serves poor neighborhoods, the craftsperson building furniture in an area not zoned for manufacturing activity, the immigrant woman reading pap smears or sewing teddy bears in a poorly lit suburban garage, and the unlicensed African street vendor are all participating in the burgeoning informal economy that characterizes a global city like New York.[22]

To enforce heretofore overlooked city regulations, then, is to crack down on the informal economy.

Early talk from Giuliani and Bratton led to much speculation among West African vendors on 125th Street. Would Giuliani act quickly to close down a market that was in gross violation of New York City ordinances? In the spring of 1994 more rumors swept down the 125th Street sidewalks: Commissioner Bratton was organizing an immanent police action; Mayor Giuliani would soon issue an order to relocate the vendors to 126th Street and St. Nicholas Avenue.

As it turned out, the beginning of the Giuliani administration did not mean the immediate end of the African market. The market, in fact, expanded in February and March of 1994, usually a slow season. Reeling from pervasive political instability as well as the World Bank's January 1994 decision to devalue the West African franc, new waves of West African immigrants arrived in New York looking for commercial opportunities. They quickly found places for themselves at the African market. On some weekends as many as 1000 vendors, according to some Harlemites quoted in the *New York Times*, might line the sidewalks of 125th Street.[23] Some of the vendors reacted to these rumors with anger. "I will never move from here. No one will go over there to buy our goods."[24] Others reacted with the equanimity of pragmatic Muslim traders. "We are here to do business. If they decide to move us, we will go. We will be all right wherever they send us. We are here to make money, not to cause trouble."[25]

In July 1994, the Masjid Malcolm Shabazz erected a large sign

on an abandoned lot on the northeast corner of 116th Street
and Lenox Avenue. It read: "Coming Soon, Masjid Malcolm
Shabazz International Plaza." The sign listed the following spon-
sors: the Masjid Malcolm Shabazz, the Harlem Business Alliance, the Harlem Urban Development Corporation, Community Board #10, and the 125th Street Vendors Association.

Soon after the appearance of the 116th Street sign, members of the 125th Street Vendors Association circulated a flyer
that denied their sponsorship of the International Plaza. The
flyer stated that one of the former officers of the 125th Vendors
Association was guilty of misrepresentation. When I asked the
Nigerien vendors about this political bickering, they said that it
was not uncommon for African Americans to play politics.[26]

As business leaders and elected officials of Harlem lobbied
the mayor to remove the street vendors from 125th Street,
rumors of an imminent police action circulated through the
market. Most African vendors believed that the city would eventually evict them, but not until after the summer.[27] Meanwhile
the battle lines had been drawn. Federal, state, and elected city
officials from Harlem joined forces with the Masjid Malcolm
Shabazz, the Harlem business community, and the Giuliani Administration—political groups with very different agendas. They
proposed to move the vendors to the suggested Masjid Malcolm
Shabazz International Plaza site on 116th Street and Lenox Avenue. Led by Morris Powell and backed by Louis Farrakhan's
Nation of Islam and the Reverend Al Sharpton, the 125th Street
Vendors Association, vehemently opposed this.[28]

Making good on one of his campaign promises, Mayor Giuliani said that as of October 17, 1994 street vending would no
longer be allowed on 125th Street. Several days before October 17, the Department of Business Services of the City of New
York circulated to the shoppers on 125th Street the following
notice, written in English, Spanish, and French.

TO ALL SHOPPERS ON 125TH STREET:
If you patronize the street vendors who sell on 125th Street and its immediate vicinity, then this notice is for you. Beginning Monday, October 17, 1994, street vending will no longer be allowed on 125th Street
and its immediate vicinity.
That's why we want you to know that as of that date (October 17, 1994)

Figure 8. Tourists observe the African Market in Harlem, summer 1993.

all of the street vendors carrying your favorite goods will be operating from two new markets at the corners of 116th Street and Lenox and 117th Street and Lenox.

The new markets are only a few blocks away and they offer many conveniences and advantages over 125th Street.

For instance:

* the markets will be cleaner.
* the vendors will be more organized.
* because of the markets, there will be less over-crowded sidewalks on 125th street.
* less overcrowded sidewalks should help reduce the opportunity for crime and the dangers posed to your safety.
* you can shop in an environment of relative comfort. You can buy your usual goods from the same vendors at no more than the usual prices.

So please, beginning October 17, 1994, bear in mind where your vendors whom you've always patronized will be at new markets on 116th and 117th Streets and Lenox Avenue; sponsored by the Malcolm Shabazz Masjid.

Your vendors in their new location need you now more than ever! Help make them a success.²⁹

I showed a copy of this notice to several West African vendors. They scoffed at City Hall's plan. One vendor theorized that the shoppers would never frequent the 116th Street market. "It's too far away [from the shopping district], and there is nothing there except crack houses and thieves. I will never go there."³⁰ Other vendors took a more circumspect attitude. A Malian vendor said that the move to 116th Street was nothing more than a plot to make money for the Masjid Malcolm Shabazz and their putative Senegalese cohorts. "The Senegalese see this move as a way to crush the other West African competition and make much money for themselves."³¹ On 125th Street vendors did not pay for their spaces, which meant that the City of New York did not receive tax revenues from them—the very definition of informal economic enterprise. Under the plan sponsored by the Giuliani administration and the Masjid Malcolm Shabazz, the vendors would pay a flat fee of $100 to register legally. They would also pay a fee of $7.00 per day for their spaces, each of which would be marked by painted lines and numbers. City Hall agreed to take only 30 percent of these revenues, leaving 70 percent to the Masjid Malcolm Shabazz.³²

Two days before Mayor Giuliani's police action, West African vendors speculated about the plans the Masjid Malcolm Shabazz had for them. All the vendors I talked to suggested that the 116th Street site was temporary. "We'll be there for only one year," one vendor predicted. "By that time, the Masjid will have gotten enough money to build a new mosque on the site. What will happen to us then?"³³ This view was underscored by Lance Shabazz, who on October 17 told Jonathan Hicks of the *New York Times* that the Masjid would build a mosque at the 116th Street site. "So this [the open-air market at 116th Street] is just a temporary arrangement. . . . When the new mosque is built, what's going to happen to the vendors then? I don't think the city has considered any of this."³⁴

On the eve of Mayor Giuliani's police action, Morris Powell, head of the 125th Street Vendors Association, was defiant, saying that his members planned to stay put "even if they bring in the National Guard. We're not going anywhere."³⁵ For their part, the NYPD seemed determined to control the public order by maintaining a high profile. "We're going to have a sufficient contingent to make sure that public safety is maintained," Assistant Chief of Police Wilbur Chapman told the *New York Post*.[36] Police also mentioned that vendors who defied the Mayor's order to leave 125th Street might face arrest and fines as high as $1000.

Meanwhile, an ad hoc group, "The Concerned People for the Development of Harlem," which did not identify its membership, underscored the issue of race in the politics of the African market. They circulated a flyer that put Asian and white store owners on notice.

If we are not allowed to do business among our own people, then we're not going to allow any other non-black entity to continue to exploit our consumer market. If our children don't eat we will make damn sure your children don't eat off our people's spending power.[37]

The imminence of the police action prompted many West African vendors to speculate about their economic future in New York City. For several days they had been meeting among themselves to discuss their options. Some of them vowed to march in the streets to protest Mayor Giuliani's decision. Others took a wait-and-see attitude. Perhaps the market at 116th Street would work out—if only temporarily. Still other West Africans thought of economic alternatives. One man said he would move his business to Canal Street in Lower Manhattan. Another said that he would seek a Work Authorization Card and move to Greensboro, North Carolina to find work in a factory. Most of the vendors I talked to expressed a kind of cynical resignation. "We have no power here. What is our choice? We do not want trouble. We will make the best of a bad situation."[38]

Policing Space

October 17, 1994. There are no vendors on the street. They have been replaced by fleets of blue paddy wagons and police vans. Men dressed in suits walk along the sidewalks, talking into walkie-talkies. The clatter of hoofs announces the arrival of a contingent of mounted police. Young men and women with

Press IDs walk stiffly up and down the street, taking photos and writing notes. Older Harlemites make the scene carrying their own video cameras and notebooks. One man says that he wants to make sure that the police action is properly documented.

At 10:00 A.M. the police block off 125th Street and Lenox Avenue. Shortly thereafter a group of demonstrating vendors, mostly African Americans, begin their march down 125th Street. Carrying the tri-colored Garveyite flag, they chant: "No food. No Peace." Considering the throngs of street vendors normally on 125th Street, the number of demonstrators seems slim — perhaps 150 of them. They are literally surrounded by police — in vans, paddy wagons, on foot, on horseback. The demonstrators form a core which the police seal off. Encircled by the police, the demonstrators move slowly down 125th Street. "No Food, No Peace." Although most of the demonstrators seem to be African Americans, a few West Africans join in.

The demonstrators gather on the plaza of the Adam Clayton Powell Building. Morris Powell, short, gray, and formless in his military fatigues, stands on a platform to speak. He is wearing a kente cloth hat and beads. A motley group gathers around him: vendors, a few Korean and Japanese tourists, a smattering of white civil servants, and people from the neighborhood, many of them older African Americans who carry cameras and camcorders.

Mr. Powell begins to speak and immediately injects the issue of race into his discourse. "We will not move," he said. "We have a right to be here. We must stop the move of whites to take over 125th Street." Another speaker talks of police racism and brutality. He says there is a conspiracy to rob African Americans of their own self-determination. He says the cops are nothing less than the Gestapo and that Mayor Giuliani is a disgrace. A woman stands up to speak. She, too, talks about the realities of racism in America, saying that African Americans need to feed their own children before letting other people feed their children with our dollars.

Someone gives Mr. Powell a bullhorn. He asks the demonstrators to begin marching in an orderly fashion. Soon thereafter, Mr. Powell is arrested for the unauthorized use of a bullhorn. Police arrest 21 other demonstrators, some of whom knocked down barriers and confronted store owners.

After the rally and arrests, the crowd disperses, but the police remain in force, strolling the sidewalks. Except for fast food restaurants, all the businesses along 125th Street are shuttered. After his arrest, Mr. Powell vows to continue to boycott "non-black owned stores."[39] On the other side, Chief of Patrol Louis Anemone says, "We'll be here forever, if necessary."[40]

Following the rally, I talked with some of the West African vendors. Many of them did not leave their apartments on the morning of October 17. One man from Niger, who sells handbags, sees the crackdown in purely economic terms. He pooh-poohs the racial discourse of African American politics in Harlem, suggesting that the crackdown on 125th Street devolved from the Masjid Malcolm Shabazz's economic interests. Indeed, if the Masjid received weekly rents from 400 vendors, it would significantly increase the religious organization's revenues. "Why should I pay them $7 per day and a $100 license fee so they can collect money to build a mosque? I refuse to go there."[41] This same Nigerien suggests that the Masjid Malcolm Shabazz International Plaza would be an absolute failure. "Just see how many people show up there today."

Boycotted Space

As promised, the 125th Street Vendors Association attempted to boycott non-black owned and run businesses on 125th Street. Supported by Louis Farrakhan, the Rev. Al Sharpton, and Nation of Islam Minister Khalid Muhammed, the vendors set up picket lines in front of these businesses. On October 18, police arrested Sharpton for illegally selling Bibles on 125th Street. On subsequent days, pickets lambasted black shoppers for frequenting white and Asian owned stores. Perhaps many of the shoppers grasped the irony that at least some of the picketers missed: the forces behind the crackdown had less to do with racial politics than with economic incentive. Consider the commentary of E. R. Shipp in the *New York Daily News*:

This week, picketers—egged on by the likes of Khalid Muhammed—are spending their days outside stores they say are owned by whites and Koreans, shouting slogans like "Close 'em down" and berating anyone who insists on shopping rather than acceding to their boycott.

They miss the point: It's not just whites and Koreans who want to

Figure 9. Africans Display "Africana" on 125th Street, summer 1993.

bring some semblance of order to the chaos on 125th St., Harlem's main commercial strip. Indeed, it's downright insulting when Powell and his ilk ignore the fact that black business, civic and political leaders have been after the mayor—from Koch to Dinkins to Giuliani—to do something about the situation. Giuliani took his sweet time, but he's finally listening to responsible Harlemites.[42]

Writing in the *New York Amsterdam News*, Abiola Sinclair took a position more moderate than that of either Powell or Shipp. Sinclair has bought from both black and Asian store owners as well as street vendors. She supports the right of the vendors to be on 125th Street, but believes they should be regulated.

My position is they should be regulated. Not in front of bus stops, hydrants, etc. Not blocking the sidewalk to the extent that people can't pass by. They should also be ticketed for keeping a dirty space. I've seen Africans and African-Americans set up in the morning, leave the spot dirty, and they pay it no attention. They leave it that way or worse. Those large concrete tubs were meant for flowers not trash.[43]

Such official talk about order as opposed to chaos, cleanliness as opposed to trashy clutter, and regulation as opposed to informality partially recapitulates the mainstream discourse of the Fifth Avenue Merchants Association in their successful attempt to clear Midtown of Senegalese "clutter" in 1985. Such discourse seeks to replace Third World chaos, filth, and informality with First World order, cleanliness, and regulation.

Given the diversity of political opinion, racial ideology, and spatial preferences about the dispersal of the African market, it was hardly surprising that the boycott had mixed results. Four days after the police action, Commissioner William J. Bratton visited 125th Street and said that he was pleased that the picketing vendors had not denied shoppers access to stores. He vowed to maintain the considerable police presence as long as necessary and said—to counter charges of police racism—that similar vending regulations would be enforced in other parts of the city. "It's getting cold," he said. "I believe nature will end up controlling the situation."[44]

By the fourth day of the 125th Street boycott the number of picketers had dwindled, the vendors had gone, the crowds had left. Even though the police profile was still high, their behavior remained very low key. Before the crackdown, according to a *New York Times* editorial,

Legitimate businesses faced obstructed doorways, summonses for dirty sidewalks and unfair competition from vendors who paid neither rent nor taxes. . . .

However, with the congestion problem solved, the city and the local business association need to consider whether 125th Street has been swept clean of street life. On a recent sunny afternoon, strollers and shoppers were sparse. If thin foot traffic becomes persistent, shop owners could find themselves scrambling to bring back the crowds.

One solution might be to find an abandoned building or lots nearer the business district where manageable numbers of legal vendors can be lodged. Harlem is a tourist stop, after all. Too little foot traffic is just as damaging as too much.[45]

The 125th Street Vendors Association boycott of non-black owned businesses petered out in less than a week. Many forces worked against its success. First, many Harlemites, who felt that the informal market had disrupted commerce on 125th Street, supported the dispersal of the street vendors. Even those like Abiola Sinclair who supported the vendors believed that they should be spatially regulated. And, like many other Harlemites, Sinclair disagreed with a logic that connected the mayoral crackdown to the boycott of non-black owned businesses. Second, the vendors, like anyone in New York City, needed income. Some of them, including many West Africans, relocated their unlicensed operations to other parts of the city, including Canal Street, Chambers Street, and 14th Street between Sixth and Fifth Avenues. The great majority of people I knew from 125th Street, however, rented stalls at the new market on 116th Street and Lenox Avenue run by the Masjid Malcolm Shabazz.

Space, Power, and Embodied Positionings

Space is a subject with a long history in anthropology. For theorists such as Lévi-Strauss, spatial relations replicate dual social orders.[46] For others, space constitutes a kind of social text that unlocks the mysteries of social meaning. Indeed, most anthropological analyses of space assume the isomorphism of space, place, and culture—all logically arranged on a homogeneous "field" of social relations. Akhil Gupta and James Ferguson note:

> The fiction of cultures as discrete, object-like phenomena occupying discrete spaces becomes implausible for those who inhabit borderlands. Related to border inhabitants are those who live a life of border-crossings—migrant workers, nomads, and members of the transnational business elite.[47]

Gupta and Ferguson might have also included participants in informal economies in such transnational spaces as the African market on 125th Street. Such commodification of transnational spaces has

> rendered any strictly bounded sense of community or locality obsolete. At the same time it has enabled the creation of forms of solidarity and identity that do not rest on the appropriation of space where contiguity and face-to-face contact are paramount.[48]

Indeed, the static notion of space is rendered superfluous by what David Harvey calls the "condition of postmodernity," which has given rise to the implosion of space and time, the explosion of mass migration, and the erosion of national boundaries.[49] It is no longer unusual to see men from rural West African villages in Harlem, hawking T-shirts emblazoned with Malcolm's "X."[50] These men transformed the 125th Street corridor into the African market, where Ghanaian "kente" hats, sewn by Koreans in Chinatown from fabric manufactured by Asians in New Jersey, were sold by Nigeriens and Malians—who do not wear such items—to African Americans for whom the hats embody an "authentic" African identity. Indeed, the West African vendors of Harlem demonstrate daily "the ability of people to confound the established spatial orders, either through physical movement or through their own conceptual and political acts of re-imagination."[51]

In this chapter I have attempted to describe the multiplicities of a public sphere in urban America. I have done so because the African market in Harlem confounds business-as-usual social analysis and compels a senuous scholarship. As we have seen, at the African market the political, the cultural and religious intentionalities of West Africans, African Americans, local elected officials, and local government bodies are articulated in a variety of conflicting spatial practices and ideologies many of which are sensuously embodied in commodities. In New York City many Third World spatial, social, and religious practices, which are themselves inextricably inter-connected, have taken *place* in spaces zoned, "First World"—all of which creates spatial arenas of multiple contestation and struggle. This chapter is one example of how and why it is important for scholars to acknowledge and confront the sensuous dimensions of transnationalism and adapt our theoretical and methodological orientations to one incontestable fact: the study of complex spaces like the African market in Harlem requires fresh epistemological and representational strategies.[52] Such study

requires a geographic sensibility, the interpretive flair of the humanist and literary theorist, and the ethnographic turn of the anthropologist and social historian. This is a tall order, I realize. But how else are we to grasp the "extraordinary crazy quilt" (Soja 1989:245), "the dazzling . . . patchwork mosaic" (Soja 1989:245; see also Davis 1990) that is the postmodern hyperspace of Los Angeles? Or the unimaginable complexity of the galactic metropolis that is Sao Paulo?[53]

To describe such complexity is, as Watts says, "a tall order" which requires, I think, a great deal of the kind of epistemological flexibility that I advocate in this book. Perhaps the best way to comprehend contemporary urban hybridity is not only to theorize about transnationalism, but to adopt the sensuously contoured epistemological suppleness demonstrated everyday by West African traders on the streets of New York City. Their ability to unite effortlessly the disparate elements of the contemporary world should be a lesson to us all.

* * *

Moussa Abdulramane sells silver rings and compact disks at the Masjid Malcolm Shabazz Harlem Market at 116th Street and Lenox Avenue. He always burns incense in the stall, and its smell makes me think of the Grande Marché in Niamey, Niger. One day I asked him why he burned incense.

"I like it," he said. "It is also good for business. It reminds my clients that I'm an African. I think they like that. And things

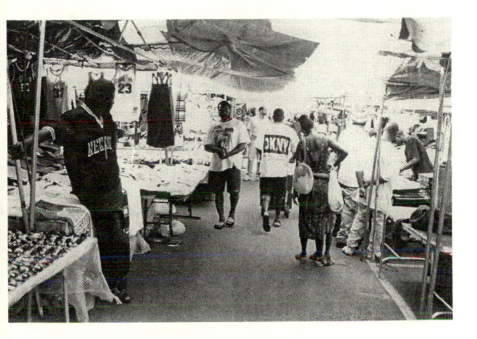

Figure 10. Vendors and shoppers at the Harlem market, 116th Street
and Lenox Avenue, summer 1996. Photo: Jasmin Tahmaseb
McConatha.

that remind the African Americans about Africa are good for
business."

In the past, Moussa sold African art in Abidjan, Ivory Coast,
but frequently traveled to Canada and the United States. On a
trip to the United States in 1993, someone stole his entire inventory, stranding him in New York City. Destitute, he sought
out his compatriots in Harlem, who provided informal credit to
buy inventory. He wanted to turn quick profits in Harlem so he
bought Malcolm X baseball caps and T-shirts as well as reggae
and rap audio cassettes. Embodying Africa along the major
thoroughfare of African American culture, Moussa set up his
table on 125th Street, quickly paid off his loan, and diversified
his inventory.

After the demise of the 125th Street market in October 1994,
he moved his stall to 116th Street. He continued to sell audio

casettes and compact disks, but also started to invest in silver rings and chains. "Malcolm X doesn't sell so well now, but they like all this silver," he said. "So I buy it. Besides, the margin of profit is higher."

By the winter of 1995–96, Moussa sold only a smattering of cassettes and CD's. He proudly showed me his extensive collection of silver jewelry. A ring with a Ghanaian Akwaba figure on it attracted my attention, for the frequently seen wooden Akwaba doll is a well-known symbol of Africa. "Do these rings come from Ghana?" I asked.

Moussa smiled. "No, I buy them cheap from Asians on Canal Street."

"Canal Street? Then the Asians must get these rings from Ghana, right?"

"No, no," Moussa said. "Actually these African rings are made in Mexico."

"Good for business?"

"Very good."

6
ARTAUD, ROUCH, AND THE CINEMA OF CRUELTY

Sensuous scholarship may well have begun in 1954 in the film theater of the Musée de l'Homme. A select audience of African and European intellectuals has been assembled to see a film screening. Marcel Griaule is there, as are Germaine Dieterlen, Paulin Vierya, Alioune Sar, and Luc de Heusch. Jean Rouch, a pioneer of ethnographic film and cinéma vérité, is in the projection booth. He beams onto the screen the initial frames of *Les maîtres fous*. Rouch begins to speak, but soon senses a rising tension in the theater. As the reel winds down, the uncompromising scenes of *Les maîtres fous* make people in the audience squirm in their seats. Rouch asks his select audience for their reaction to the film.

Marcel Griaule, Rouch's mentor in anthropology, says that the film is a travesty; he tells Rouch to destroy it. In rare agreement with Griaule, Paulin Vierya, an African filmmaker, also suggests that the film be destroyed. There is only one encouraging reaction to *Les maîtres fous*, that of fellow anthropologist Luc de Heusch.[1]

This reaction clearly wounded Jean Rouch. Should he destroy this film? In filming *Les maîtres fous* Rouch's intentions were far from racist; he wanted to demonstrate how Songhay people in the colonial Gold Coast embodied knowledge and practices "not yet known to us." Just as in one of his earlier films, *Les magiciens de Wanzerbé* (1947), in which a sorcerer defies commonsense expectations by vomiting and then swallowing a small metal chain of power, so in *Les maîtres fous*, Rouch wanted to document the unthinkable—that men and women possessed by the Hauka spirits, the spirits of French and British colonialism, can handle fire and dip their hands into boiling cauldrons of sauce without burning themselves. Always the provocateur, Rouch wanted to challenge his audiences sensuously to think new thoughts about Africa and Africans. Could these people of Africa possess knowledge "not yet known to us," a veritable challenge to racist European conceptions of Africa's place in the history of science?

Perhaps Rouch's intent in *Les maîtres fous* was naive. The brutal images overpower the film's subtle philosophical themes. After other screenings to selected audiences in France, Rouch decided on a limited distribution—to art theaters and film festivals.

Rouch was troubled by such criticism, for his prior practices and commitments were clearly anti-racist, anti-colonialist, and anti-imperialist. Critics have suggested that the controversy surrounding *Les maîtres fous* compelled Rouch to make films, especially his films of "ethno-fiction," which more directly confronted European racism and colonialism. Such a view may well be correct, for after *Les maîtres fous* Rouch made a series of films that portrayed the political and cultural perniciousness of European ethnocentrism and colonialism in the 1950s. But Rouch's political films are not simply the result of his reaction to stinging criticism, they also embody, in my view, a cinematic extension of Artaud's notion of the theater of cruelty. In a cinema of cruelty the filmmaker's goal is not to recount per se, but to present an array of unsettling images that seek to transform the audience psychologically and politically. In the remainder of this chapter I first discuss the Artaudian theories of the cinema and theater and speculate about the contours of a cinema of cruelty. I then use those contours to analyze four of Rouch's more politically and philosophically conscious films, *Jaguar* (1953–67), *Moi, un noir* (1957), *La pyramide humaine* (1959), and *Petit à petit* (1969). I conclude with a discussion of how a cinema of cruelty is a lesson in sensuous scholarship.

Artaud and the Cinema

Throughout his life Antonin Artaud (1896–1948) suffered from long bouts of incoherence—the result of schizophrenia and drug addictions. Despite these difficulties, Artaud broke into the theater as an actor in 1921. Between 1921 and 1924 he joined the experimental repertory company of Charles Dullin, for whom he acted and designed sets and costumes. He also acted with Georges and Ludmilla Pitoefs, who produced plays by Blok, Shaw, Pirondello, Capek, and Molnar. During this period, Artaud also began to write plays, essays, poems, manifestoes, and film scenarios. In 1925 he joined André Breton and other Surrealists contributing essays to the review *The Surrealist Revolution.* Between 1926 and 1929, he, Roger Vitrac, and Robert Aron founded the Théâtre Alfred Jarry, which briefly became of center of the avant-garde stage in France. After three years of meticulous planning in the early 1930s, Artaud opened his short-lived Theater of Cruelty. The failure of this experiment did not dampen his creative spirit, for he traveled widely and continued to write plays, essays, and manifestoes. In 1938 his influential book of essays, *The Theatre and Its Double,* was published. Critics hailed it as an important work. This recognition, however, did not exorcise Artaud's existential demons. He spent much of the last part of his life in asylums.[2]

In Paris, Artaud was quickly drawn to the magic of the cinema, the subject of many of his early essays, especially during his tenure as director of the Bureau de Recherches Surréalistes. Like Robert Desnos, Artaud penned many film scenarios (only one was ever produced). He wrote scenarios not to sell his ideas to producers but to explore his thoughts about the relationship between films and dreams.[3] Like other Surrealists, Artaud found an affinity between dreams and the cinema, and his analyses of film, according to Linda Williams, probed this relationship with great sensitivity.[4] Unlike Robert Desnos, who unproblematically accepted a link between the experience of dreams and film, Artaud focused on how film signifies.

In Artaud's writings on film, his great enemy is language, for it is language's arbitrary connection of things (referents) to sequences of sound that stifles the human imagination. According to Linda Williams, "What Artaud wanted was a language that would not only *express*, but also—impossibly—*be* the very flesh and blood of his thought."[5] Artaud saw film as a possible means of escaping the perils of linguistic signification. Williams goes on to suggest a link between Artaud's cinematic theories and Christian Metz's notion of the imaginary signifier.

The notion of the immediacy of film, of its ability to bypass the usual coded channels of language through a visual short circuit that acts "almost intuitively on the brain," is Artaud's attempt to rediscover what he terms the primitive arrangement of things. . . . For the film image, unlike an accumulation of words on the page or an enactment of these words in a theater, cannot be pointed to as a thing that is actually *there*. In other words, the film (as Christian Metz has shown, but as the Surrealists had already intuited) is an *imaginary signifier*. . . . Briefly, the term refers to the paradoxical fact that, although film is the most perceptual of all the arts and even though its signifier (the play of light and shadow on the screen representing objects of the real world) gives a powerful impression of reality, this impression is only an illusion.[6]

As Artaud recognized, human beings are lulled into accepting the reality of the images in dreams and films; they "misrecognize" the illusion of the image. The scenarios of Artaud and Desnos, as mentioned in Chapter 4, attempted to construct films that would deconstruct our fundamental relationship to the image. In this way, film could be a means of unveiling the fundamental structure of the unconscious thereby liberating it from the tyranny of language.[7]

Artaud and the Theater of Cruelty

By the time of the publication of André Breton's *Second Surrealist Manifesto* (1929), Artaud had become less enamored of the cinema and its revolutionary possibilities. "Movies in their turn, murdering us with second-hand reproductions which, filtered through machines, cannot unite with our sensibility, have maintained us for ten years in an ineffectual torpor, in which all of our faculties appear to be foundering."[8] Perhaps Artaud realized that the seductive qualities of the cinema can also create a kind of anesthetized state that promotes inactivity (see Chapter 4).[9] Artaud may have recognized that the cinema's immediacy was not immediate enough for his revolutionary program of social transformation.

In time Artaud turned more and more of his attentions to the theater, specifically to his Theater of Cruelty. Considering the impact his writings have had on the theory and practice of theater in the twentieth century, it is ironic that his great dramatic experiment closed only two weeks after it opened in June of 1935. The "cruelty" of the productions apparently nauseated audiences.

Like other aspects of Artaud's voluminous work, his writings on the Theater of Cruelty are fragments, jagged puzzle pieces that never form a coherent whole. Artaud's early experience in the Parisian theater disillusioned him. He reviled so-called masterpieces: "One of the reasons for the asphyxiating atmosphere in which we live without possible escape or remedy . . . is our respect for what has been written, formulated, or painted, what has been given form." [10] In fact, Artaud felt that the literary staidness of the cerebral arts was socially unhealthy.

Masterpieces of the past are good for the past: they are not good for us. We have the right to say what has been said and even what has not been said in a way that belongs to us, a way that is immediate and direct, corresponding to present modes of feeling, and understandable to everyone. [11]

For Artaud, the Theater of Cruelty was the solution to social asphyxiation, for it constituted a space of transformation in which people could be reunited with their life forces, with the poetry that lies beyond the poetic text. [12] More specifically, the Theater of Cruelty

means a theater difficult and cruel for myself first of all. And on the level of performance, it is not the cruelty we can exercise upon each other by hacking at each other's bodies, carving up our personal anatomies . . . but the much more terrible and necessary cruelty which things can exercise against us. We are not free. And the sky can still fall on our heads. And the theater has been created to teach us that first of all. [13]

In some respects Artaud yearned for what he saw as the participatory theatrics of non-Western rituals which foregrounded transformative spectacle. According to Artaud, that idea of theater had long been lost. He traced this loss to Shakespeare and Racine and the advent of psychological theater, which separates the audience from the immediacy of "violent" activity. The advent of the cinema compounded this loss.[14]

It is clear from Artaud's comments about myth, spectacle, and "theatrical violence" that his vision for the Theater of Cruelty was inspired by pre-theatrical rituals in which powerful symbols were employed for therapeutic ends. In his first manifesto on the Theater of Cruelty, Artaud wrote:

> But by an altogether Oriental means of expression, this objective and concrete language of the theater can fascinate and ensnare the organs. It flows into the sensibility. Abandoning Occidental uses of speech, it turns words into incantation. It extends the voice. It utilizes the vibrations and qualities of voice. It wildly tramples rhythms underfoot. It pile-drives sounds. It seeks to exalt, to benumb, to charm, to arrest the sensibility. It liberates a new lyricism of gesture which, by its precipitation or its amplitude in the air, ends by surpassing the lyricism of words. It ultimately breaks away from the intellectual subjugation of language, by conveying the sense of a new and deeper intellectuality which hides itself beneath gestures and signs, raised to the dignity of particular exorcisms.[15]

Although Artaud disassociated himself from the Surrealists in the late 1920s, the influence of Surrealism twists its way through his writing: the suspicion of logic, language, and rationality; the use of the arts to liberate the power of human vitality from the repressed unconscious; the promotion of social revolution; the juxtaposition of "primitive" and "civilized" imagery to create transformative poetry.[16]

Artaud's writings on the Theater of Cruelty also evoke spirit possession rituals. Albert Bermel, an Artaud critic, suggests that the rites associated with the Corybantes, a pre-Socratic Greek secret society, are quite similar to those proposed for the Theater of Cruelty. Through music and dance, he claims, the Corybantes initiates were whipped into a frenzy, a crazed state that was expiated through purification rituals, "an experience not dissimilar in kind to the one Artaud seems to have had in mind."[17]

Bermel is not the only scholar to suggest links between ritual and theater. Gilbert Rouget argues that classical Greek theater evolved from the Corybantes, which he calls a possession cult.[18] Other French scholars have proposed links among possession, poetry, and theater.[19] The Artaudian scenario outlined for the Theater of Cruelty also bears striking resemblance to many West African possession rituals, including those practiced by the Songhay in the Republic of Niger—the subjects of most of Jean Rouch's films.[20]

Rouch and the Cinema of Cruelty

It is clear that Artaud believed that the Theater of Cruelty could not be transferred from stage to screen. Although he was fascinated by the cinema in his earlier writings, his interests gradually gravitated toward the more ritualized framework of the theater. Given Artaud's dispositions, is a cinema of cruelty possible? Like the sets and costumes of Artaud's shortlived Theater of Cruelty, the images of the great Surrealist films wage war against culturally conditioned perception. Films like *Un chien andalou* (1929) and *L'âge d'or* (1930) play with generally recognized patterns of perception, namely, the illusion that that which is patently unreal (the images of the cinema) is in fact real. Surrealist film, following the argument of Linda Williams, exposes the illusion—some would say, delusion—of the perceptual processing of imaginary signifiers.[21] Artaud's scenarios, in fact, dwell on themes that expose the "misrecognition" of the cinematic image. In this sense, Surrealist film meets some of the criteria of Artaud's Theater of Cruelty. But are these films transformative? Do they alter behavior? Do they purify the spirit? Do they release pent-up vitality?

Although the cinema can seduce us into highly personalized but relatively inactive dreamlike states, its culturally coded images can at the same time trigger anger, shame, sexual excitement, revulsion, and horror. Artaud wanted to transform his audiences by tapping their unconscious through the visceral presence of sound and image, flesh and blood. He wanted to revert to what André Schaeffner called the "pre-theater," a ritualized arena of personal transformation, a project for a ritualized stage.[22]

Although Jean Rouch has concentrated his artistic efforts exclusively on the cinema, his path shares much with that of Artaud. Like Artaud, he was very much influenced by the sensuousness of Surrealism. In his various interviews, both published and broadcast, he often paid homage to the Surrealists. When Rouch witnessed his first possession ceremony among the Songhay of Niger in 1942, it evoked for him the writings of Breton and the poems of Eluard.[23] Perhaps the vitality of Songhay possession rituals, a virtual pre-theater—compelled Rouch to make "cruel" films. In some of his films, especially those he refers to as "ethno-fiction," he pursues an Artaudian path. He always tells a story in his films, but the narratives in these films are secondary to his philosophical intent. In these films Rouch wants to transform his viewers. He wants to challenge their cultural assumptions. He wants the audience—still mostly European and North American—to confront its ethnocentrism, its repressed racism, its latent primitivism.

Anyone who has been assailed by the brutal images of *Les maîtres fous* has experienced Rouch's cinema of cruelty. In *Les maîtres fous* "Rouch's path is correct not only because he doesn't ignore colonialism, but because leaving constantly his own environs and exhibiting nature through the massive effects she produces elsewhere, it at no time allows the spectator to remain indifferent, but compels him in some way if not to take a position, at least to change."[24] *Les maîtres fous* evokes the meaning of decolonization: that European decolonization must begin with individual decolonization—the decolonization of a person's thinking, of a person's "self." Such an effect is clearly an element of a Cinema of Cruelty, a cinema that uses humor as well as unsettling juxtapositions to jolt the audience.

Jaguar

Jaguar is not an insufferably "cruel" film; rather, it is infused with what Italo Calvino once called the brilliance of "lightness." I like to call *Jaguar* "*Tristes tropiques*, African style"—with a very significant twist. Like *Tristes tropiques* and other works in the picaresque tradition, *Jaguar* is a tale of adventure, a story of initiation into the wonders of other worlds and other peoples. The protagonists, Damoré, a "petit bandit," Lam, a Fulan shepherd, and Illo, a Niger River fisherman, learn a great deal from their adventures in the colonial Gold Coast. The difference between *Tristes tropiques* and *Jaguar*, however, is an important one. We expect Claude Lévi-Strauss to be enlightened by his voyage to Brazil. But do we expect the same for three young Nigeriens from Ayoru or from Nigerien street vendors selling Africana in Harlem? Can Others embark on philosophical journeys of Enlightenment? In *Jaguar*, Rouch forces us to confront a wide array of colonialist assumptions: that in their "backwardness" all Africans are alike; that in their "backwardness" Africans have no sense of the wanderlust; that in their "backwardness" Africans do not extract wisdom from their journeys. With great humor, *Jaguar* shatters our expectations. Along their journey to the colonial Gold Coast, the Others (Damoré, Lam, and Illo) confront their own Others: the Gurmantche who file their teeth into sharp points and drink millet beer; the Somba who eat dog and shun clothing. At the Somba market Damoré says to Lam:

"Mais, il sont complètement nus, mon vieux." [They are completely nude, old man.]
"Complètement," says Lam. [Completely]

For Lam, Illo, and Damoré such a corporeal display is unthinkable. They have encountered the "primitive's primitive," thus affirming Montaigne's affirmation that "each man calls barbarism whatever is not his own practice; for indeed, it seems we have no other test of truth and reason than the example and pattern of opinions and customs of the country we live in."[25]

Later in *Jaguar*, Damoré becomes very "jaguar" ("with it"), Lam becomes a small time entrepreneur (*nyama izo*—the children of disorder), and Illo toils as a laborer in the port of Accra. At all junctures in the film, difference is underscored: distinctions are made between northerners and southerners, Christians and Muslims, traditionalists and moderns. In *Jaguar*, Africa is not a continent of sameness; it is rather a land of finite distinctions, a space for the politics of difference. Commenting critically on Kwame Nkruma and his cronies, Damoré says:

"Ils sont bien nourris, ceux-la." [These ones are well nourished]

A political commentary of visionary proportions, for the leaders of newly independent Africa would become very well nourished, indeed—fed by the political systems they created.

And so in *Jaguar* Africa emerges from the shadows of sameness and is cast into the swift cross-currents of political fragmentation. Rouch's protagonists, like Susan Sontag's Lévi-Strauss, are heros—adventurers in a heterogeneous Africa who confront their own primitives as well as the stormy politics of their epoch. As such, these wise and articulate "Others" defy our expectations and make us ponder our own categories of sameness and difference, civilized and primitive. In this way, Rouch uses *Jaguar* critically to juxtapose Europe and Africa.

Like the Artaudian wanderer, Rouch's "fictional" wanderers in *Jaguar* challenge the cultural assumptions of viewers, forcing them to confront the centuries-old legacy of European ethnocentrism and racism. *Jaguar* makes us laugh as it subverts the primitivist imagery of Africa. True to a cinema of cruelty, *Jaguar* compels viewers to decolonize their thinking, their "selves."

Moi, un noir

To make *Jaguar*, Rouch employed his friends as actors. Although Damoré, Lam, and Illo acted well in the film, they had never been migrants. While he was editing *Jaguar*, Rouch asked Oumarou Ganda to attend a screening. Ganda, who *had* been a migrant in Abidjan, challenged Rouch to make a film about real migrants like himself. Rouch took up Ganda's challenge, which resulted in *Moi, un noir*, one of the first films, ethnographic or otherwise, that depicted the pathos of life in changing Africa. In the film, we follow Ganda and his compatriots as they work as dockers in the port of Abidjan. We see how hard they work, how little they are paid, and how they are belittled as human beings. We see how work and life steal from them the last vestiges of their dignity. In this space of deprivation and demoralization, we are touched by Oumarou Ganda's fantasies. We are saddened by his disappointments. We are outraged by his suffering. We hear his sad voice. In this film an "invisible man" tells his sad tale. Oumarou Ganda's story enables us to see how the discourse of colonialism and racism disintegrates the human spirit. Are not the dreams of Oumarou Ganda the dreams of the oppressed—the hope against all hopes that someday one will recapture his or her dignity?

Like *Jaguar*, *Moi, un noir* is a film that obliterates the boundaries between fact and fiction, documentary and story, observation and participation, objectivity and subjectivity. Rouch calls *Moi, un noir* and *Jaguar* works of "ethno-fiction," works in which the "fiction" is based on long-term ethnographic research. In this way, both *Jaguar* and *Moi, un noir* are biting critiques of the staid academicism that pervades the university in Europe and North America. Imprisoned by eighteenth-century intellectualist assumptions in a postcolonial epoch, the academy, as I have argued in this book, was and is ill-equipped to deal with the sensuous complexities of the changing world. These films, which are also indictments of European modernity, remind us that, in a world in which expectations are continuously subverted, the sky, to paraphrase Artaud, can suddenly fall down on our heads. The intent of these films is clearly political; through the subversion of "received" categories, they challenge us to confront physiognomically our own ugliness—an exercise in Artaudian "cruelty."

La pyramide humaine

Rouch's sensuous critique of European modernity does not end with *Moi, un noir*. As he is found of saying, "one film gives birth to another." *Moi, un noir* prompted him to make another film set in Abidjan—*La pyramide humaine*. In this film, the title of which is taken from one of Paul Eluard's Surrealist poems, Rouch explores the relations between French and African students at an Abidjan high school. Here viewers observe the divergent lives of impoverished African and affluent European students. Some of the African students hate the Europeans; some of the European students are unabashedly racist. The students argue about colonialism and racism. The debate intensifies when a new female student from Paris begins to date an African. This social act, which taps the fear of interracial sexuality, unleashes a torrent of emotion and prejudice on both sides. While *Moi, un noir* focused on the plight of African migratory workers, *La pyramide humaine* sets its sights on the sexuality of interracial relations in a colonial state—a volatile topic in 1959. Not surprisingly, the film was banned in most of Francophone Africa. And yet even today it speaks eloquently to issues of the repressed fear of interracial sex and of liberal duplicity and racism in Europe and North America.

La pyramide humaine is also very conscious of its own construction. Rouch qua filmmaker appears in several sequences of the film, using his presence to carefully weave a subplot through the text. The main story involves the confrontation of two worlds, two sets of prejudices; it is about how confrontation can be transformative. The subplot recounts how the making of the film transformed the lives of the actors. The subplot, then, subverts the specious boundary between fact and fiction and shows how film constructs and transforms, how film is "cruel" in the Artaudian sense. Shot in color, this film is "cruel" indeed, for it impels viewers to acknowledge in black and white their culturally conditioned sexual fears and fantasies.

Petit à petit

"One film gives birth to another." *Moi, un noir* gave birth to *La pyramide humaine*, which gave birth to Rouch's most famous work, *Chronique d'un été*, a film about Rouch's own "tribe," les Français. In 1960 how did the French deal with difference— with Jews, Arabs, and Africans? The film, which was politically provocative, is considered a landmark in the history of the cinema for two reasons: (1) it is among the first works filmed in synchronous sound; and (2) it launched the Nouvelle Vague in French cinema. In the 1960s Rouch continued to film in Africa. He completed *The Lion Hunters* in 1964, and began to film the magnificent Sigui ceremonies of the Dogon of Mali in 1967. But he wanted to make yet another film in France and decided on Jaguar II, which he called *Petit à petit*, after the corporation formed by Damoré, Lam, and Illo in the original *Jaguar*.

The scenario of *Petit à petit* focuses on two entrepreneurs, Damoré and Lam, who want to build a luxury hotel in Niamey, Niger, which would cater exclusively to Europeans. But Damoré and Lam know nothing about Europeans. Like a good anthropologist, Damoré decides to travel to Paris to study the lifeways of the French tribe: to observe and measure them. How else would they know how to design the hotel's interiors? How else would they know how to order sofas and beds of the correct dimensions? And so Damoré flies to Paris, where he embarks on his study. But Lam becomes so worried about the impact of France on Damoré's being that he decides to join his friend in Paris. With great humor, Rouch tells the story of Damoré's and Lam's Parisian experience. As in *Jaguar*, Damoré and Lam turn the tables of our expectations. Europeans are usually the film-makers, not the filmed. Europeans are usually the observers, not the observed.

One of the most memorable scenes occurs on the Place Troca-dero, between La Musée de l'Homme and the Cinémathique Française, a space filled with academic significance. It is winter and Damoré, posing as a doctoral student, approaches several French people armed with anthropometric calipers.

"Excuse me sir," he says to an elderly gentleman, "I am a student from Africa working on my thesis at the university. Would you permit me to measure you?" With the gentleman's willing consent, Damoré measures his skull, his neck, his shoulders, chest, and waist. Damoré then approaches a young woman and again makes his request. He measures her dimensions and then asks:

"Excusez-moi, mademoiselle, mais est-ce que je pourrais voir vos dents?" [Excuse me, miss, but I can see your teeth?]

The woman opens her mouth.

"Ah oui. Très bien. Merci, mademoiselle." [Ah, yes. Very good. Thank you, miss]

There is much, much more to this film, but I describe this scene to underscore Rouch's ongoing contempt of the academy's conservatism, its uneasiness with innovation, sensu-ousness, and change. Throughout his films Rouch casts asper-sions on what he calls "academic imperialism." Such a theme blazes a "cruel" trail for scholars who believe that Reason eclipses all other approaches to social description.

And so, Rouch's films of ethno-fiction cut to the flesh and blood of European colonialist being. His films compel us to re-flect on our latent racism, our repressed sexuality, the taken-for-granted assumptions of our intellectual heritage. In so doing, Rouch's films expose the centrality of power relations to our dreams, thoughts, and actions. Such exposure is a key ingredi-ent in a cinema of cruelty.

The Poet's Path

During my research on Rouch's oeuvre I wondered why the philosophical aspects of his work—embodied in sensuous filmic images—are underappreciated in Europe and unknown in North America. Why is it that until recently contemporary critics in Europe and North America rarely, if ever, considered the pioneering work of Rouch? The answer, I think, is that most critics, philosophers, and anthropologists are still part of the academy Rouch so skillfully reproaches for its conservatism. Academics are still bound to Reason, to disembodied words, and to plain style—the antithesis of sensuous scholarship. Scholars, as I have argued in previous chapters, usually seek the discursive and eschew the figurative. Images are transformed into inscriptions that form a coherent discourse. Poetry and what Merleau-Ponty called "the indirect language" are out-of-academic bounds.

More than a generation ago Jean Rouch understood the transformative power of poetry. Many of his films are poetic in the sense recently invoked by Trinh T. Minh-ha:

> For the nature of poetry is to offer meaning in such a way that it can never end with what is said or shown, destabilizing thereby the speaking subject and exposing the fiction of all rationalization. . . . So to avoid merely falling into this pervasive world of the stereotyped and the cliched, filmmaking has all to gain when conceived as a performance that engages as well as questions (its own)language. . . . However . . . poetic practice can be "difficult" to a number of viewers, because in mainstream films and media our ability to play with meanings other than the literal ones that pervade our visual and aural environments is rarely solicited.[26]

Literalness is the curse of the academy, and yet the strong poetic undercurrents of a few films and scholarly works somehow survive.

Because of their literalness, academics are often the last people to stumble on innovation. Such is often the case in the human sciences. One of my philosopher friends admitted that professional philosophers are fifty years behind the times. For inspiration, he advised me, look to the arts. Indeed, for most of us the epistemology of plain style means that photography and film are, to use John Homiak's felicitous phrase, "images on the edge of the text."[27] In Rouch's case, this means that his films are most often judged in terms of technological innovation rather than philosophical lyricism.

A generation before the "experimental moment" in the human sciences, scores of filmmakers, artists, and poets produced works that embodied many of the themes that define the condition of postmodernity: the pathos of social fragmentation, the recognition of the impact of expanding global economies, the cultural construction of racism, the legacy of academic imperialism, the quandaries of self-referentiality, the rewards of implicated participation, the acknowledgment of heteroglossia, the permeability of categorical boundaries (fact/fiction//objectivity/subjectivity). In one of his many interviews Rouch said:

> For me, as an ethnographer and filmmaker, there is almost no boundary between documentary film and films of fiction. The cinema, the art of the double, is already a transition from the real world to the imaginary world, and ethnography, the science of thought systems of others, is a permanent crossing point from one conceptual universe to another; acrobatic gymnastics where losing one's footing is the least of the risks.[28]

Rouch used a "cruel" epistemological acrobatics to tack between the sensible and the intelligible. Perhaps the way to the future of the human sciences is to follow Rouch's "cruel" path and confront the sometimes inspiring, sometimes fearsome world of incertitude.

The sky is lower than we think. Who knows when it will crash down on our heads?

EPILOGUE

Sensuous Ways of Knowing/Living

In a kingdom of long ago, there was a dervish from a very strict school who was one day strolling along a river bank. As he walked he pondered great problems of morality and scholarship. For years he had studied the word of the Prophet. Through study of Prophet's sacred language, he reasoned, he would one day be blessed with Mohammed's divine illumination and acquire the ultimate Truth.

The dervish's ruminations were interrupted by a piercing noise: some person was incanting a dervish prayer. What is this man doing? he wondered to himself. How can he be mispronouncing the syllables? He should be saying "Ya Hu" instead of "U Ya Hu."

It was his moral duty, he thought, to correct his brother, to set him straight on the path to piety. Accordingly, he hired a boat and rowed his way to an island, the source of the errant incantation. He found a man sitting in front of a hut, dressed in frayed wool. The man swayed in time to his rhythmic repetitions. So engrossed was he in his sacred incantation that he did not hear the first dervish's approach.

"Forgive me," the first dervish said. "I was in town and heard your prayer. With all due respect, I believe you have erred in your prayer. You should say 'Ya Hu' instead of 'U Ya Hu.'"

"Thank you so much for your kindness," the second dervish said. "I appreciate what you have done."

Pleased with his good deed, the first dervish boarded his boat. Allah, he reasoned, would take notice of his pious efforts. As it was said, the one who can repeat the sacred incantation without error might one day walk on water. Perhaps one day he'd be capable of such a feat.

When the first dervish's boat reached midstream, he noticed that the second dervish had not learned his lesson well, for the latter continued to repeat the incantation incorrectly. The first dervish shook his head. At least he had made the proper effort. Lost in his thoughts, the first dervish then witnessed a bizarre sight. The bumbling second dervish walked on the water and approached the first dervish's boat.

Shocked, the first dervish stopped his rowing. The second dervish walked up to him and said: "Brother, I am sorry to trouble you, but I have to come out to ask you again the standard method of making the repetition you were telling me, because I find it difficult to remember it."[1]

*   *   *

The most important and difficult lesson that a sensuous scholarship provides is that of humility. No matter how learned we may become, no matter how deeply we have mastered a subject, the world, for the sensuous scholar, remains a wondrous place that stirs the imagination and sparks creativity. Those who struggle with humility, no matter their scholarly station, admit willingly that they have much to learn from forgetful old men and women who, at first glance, seem to have little knowledge to impart. They not only have precious knowledge to convey but can teach us much about living in the world.

Among the Songhay of Niger it is usually this kind of person who is possessed by the sacred words of history and the powerful secrets of sorcerous power. It is their humility, I think, that enables them to receive knowledge and transform it into wisdom.

The late Edmond Jabès understood the wisdom of this primary lesson of sensuous scholarship:

I see myself again in the deserts of Egypt, looking for pebbles—yellow, sometimes brown—digging them out of the sand, taking them home for the sake of the human face that would suddenly emerge out of their nothingness—an eternal human face that time had modeled for centuries, not mere moments—their face alive against life.

Along amid sand, whose every grain bears witness to an exhausted wind, a desolate world, I was satisfied with appearance, whereas it is inside the stone that the heart of death is merrily at work, where, with a beat of heaven or hell, the closed universe of eternity is written.[2]

Humility enables the sensuous scholar to confront the terrifying eternity of the social universe with the lightness of a caress, with the smile of humble comprehension. If we allow humility to work its wonders, it can bring sensuousness to our practices and expression. It can enable us to live well in the world.

NOTES

Prologue

1. Reconstructed from a story recounted in Idries Shah's *Tales of the Dervishes* (1970).
2. E. Husserl (1970).
3. M. Merleau-Ponty (1964,147).
4. S. Bordo (1987,108). See also A. Jagger and S. Bordo (1989), and S. Suleiman (1986).
5. M. Foucault (1970, 1972); T. Mitchell (1988), E. Said (1978), C. Miller (1986, 1990); G. Starett (1995).
6. P. Bourdieu (1984, 210).
7. B. Turner (1991,11).
8. This is especially the case with the *écriture féminine* movement in France. In anthropology J. Boddy (1989) is a well wrought case in point. The works of M. Taussig are important anthropological cases in point.
9. J. Butler (1990, 133–34).
10. See P. Stoller (1989b; 1995, 21–22); see also D. Howes (1991), C. Classen (1993).

Part One: Introduction

1. R. Rorty (1979, 1989, 1991).
2. D. Howes (1991).
3. P. Stoller (1989b); P. Stoller and C. Olkes (1990); C. Classen (1993).

Chapter 1: The Sorcerer's Body

1. C. Lévi-Strauss (1967).
2. This distanciation is characteristic of all of Lévi-Strauss's major works (*Mythologiques, La voie des masques*, etc.). The primary exception, of course, is *Tristes tropiques*, which, according to a 1988 interview (see Lévi-Strauss 1988), he wrote only because he thought his academic career was doomed.
3. E. Evans-Pritchard (1976, 11).
4. See M. Marwick (1952); M. Douglas (1970); J. Beattie and J. Middleton (1969).
5. H. Cixous (1976, 875).
6. See P. Stoller (1989b).
7. P. Bowles (1976, 233).

8. Ibid., 235.

9. Ibid., 312.

10. See P. Stoller and C. Olkes (1987).

11. Ibid.; see also P. Stoller (1989b).

12. See J. Rouch (1989).

13. According to Rouch, similar incidents occurred in Wanzerbé during the late 1940s and early 1950s. In one case a regional administrator, a judge, became paralyzed after visiting Wanzerbé. He was evacuated and on his return to French soil, regained the use of his limbs. Interview, March 1, 1990, Paris, France.

14. M. Jackson (1989,3).

15. Ibid., 3.

16. Ibid., 4. See also P. Kilbride and J. Kilbride (1990) on their notion of "interactive ethnography."

Chapter 2: The Griot's Tongue

1. T. Hale (1990).

2. A. Hampaté Ba (1981,166).

3. C. Bird (1971,98).

4. There is much debate about the definition of *nyama*. Sory Camara (1976,11) translates it as "all powerful spirit." Massa Makan Diabaté translated it as "evil"; others have translated it as "trash or garbage" (N'Diaye 1970,14). In Songhay the notion of "force" is not concretely articulated; "force" rather is articulated through deeds. The "force" of a sorcerer is not named but recognized through his or her *korte*, literally charms, or his or her "work."

5. C. Miller (1990, 81).

6. See J. Irvine (1978).

7. J. Chernoff (n.d., 2).

8. A. Hampaté Ba (1981).

9. R. Barthes (1977).

10. R. Barthes (1972,164–65).

11. See C. Miller (1985, 1990); V. Mudimbe (1988); E. Said (1978, 1989); G. Spivak (1990).

12. See J. Clifford (1988); G. Marcus and D. Cushman (1982); E. Said (1989); S. Tyler (1987).

13. See M. Cesara (1981); K. Dwyer (1982); M. Jackson (1986); R. Price (1983).

14. T. Beidelman (1989); K. Birth (1990); P. Sangren (1988).

15. See D. Henault (1991); D. MacDougall (1992): J. Ruby (1991); F. Ginsburg (1991); T. Turner (1991).

16. See T. Hale (1990); J. Irvine (1978); C. Miller (1990).

17. See A. Napier (1992), in which he asserts that the failure of contemporary art devolves from contemporary artists' social disembodi-

ment. Such disembodiment means that they fail to revivify things that have power in and of themselves.

18. See C. Bergé (n.d.,2).

19. P. Clastres (1974).

20. C. Bergé (n.d.,4).

21. Ibid., 5.

22. Ibid., 6.

23. R. J. Coombe (1991a).

24. R. Predal (1982,78).

25. D. MacDougall (1992).

26. See P. Stoller (1992).

27. This statement comes from a letter that David Sapir sent to prospective authors in his ongoing Culture and Symbol Series which is now published by the University of Arizona Press.

28. See J. Irvine (1978).

29. My use of plain style in this article is not at all ironic. Like the griot, the writer of scholarly essays must pay some heed to institutions and audiences by following some of the overriding realist conventions of academic publishing in the human sciences. And yet no ethnographer—even the author of a scholarly essay—needs to adhere to all scholarly conventions of representation. Ethnographers as griots can embed into their rule-governed prose performance elements that play with those very conventions, rendering them problematic.

30. See J. Fernandez (1982).

31. See J. Clifford and G. Marcus (1986); M. Manganaro (1990); G. Marcus and M. Fischer (1985); R. Rosaldo (1989); E. Said (1989); S. Tyler (1987).

32. T. Beidelman (1989,267).

33. P. Sangren (1988).

34. J. Lett (1991).

35. D. Harvey (1989).

36. K. Gergen (1991); see also Z. Bauman (1991).

37. P. Rabinow (1985); see also R. Fox (1991).

38. See G. Marcus (1990).

39. P. Rabinow (1985, 9, 12).

40. Ibid., 3.

41. R. Coombe (1991a, 115).

42. Ibid., 116.

43. E. Said (1989).

44. J. Holston (1989).

45. P. Rabinow (1989,16).

46. See J. Boddy (1989); D. Kondo (1990); K. Narayan (1989); see also R. Desjarlais (1992); D. Foley (1990, 1995); D. Rose (1987, 1989); J. Wafer (1991).

47. J. Rouch (1990).

Part Two: Introduction

1. P. Connerton (1989).

Chapter 3: Embodying Colonial Memories

1. See J-C Muller (1971); P. Stoller (1992).
2. See J. Rouch (1956).
> 3. F. Fugelstad (1975, 1983).
4. P. Stoller (1989a, 1992).
5. J. Boddy (1989); M. Lambek (1981). See also A. Napier (1992).
6. I thank Rosemary J. Coombe for clarifying this point, which is articulated elsewhere in more indirect language (P. Stoller 1989b; M. Jackson 1989).
7. P. Stoller (1989a, 1995).
8. M. Jackson (1989); P. Stoller 1989b; D. Howes (1991).
9. The literature on spirit possession is voluminous. Space precludes a thorough discussion of the strengths and weaknesses of such important studies as Bourguignon (1976); I. Lewis (1971) (functionalist); G. Obeysekere (1981); J. Monfouga-Nicholas (1972); V. Crapanzano (1973, 1980); Zempleni (1969) (psychological/psychoanalytic); A. Kehoe and D. Geletti (1981) (biological); M. Lambek (1981); J. Boddy (1989); D. Lan (1985); J. Comaroff (1985) (interpretive/textual); A. Schaeffner (1965); M. Leiris (1958); G. Rouget (1980); J-M Gibbal (1988); Stoller (1989a) (performance/theatrical). Recent studies by A. Masquelier (1991, 1993) and P. Schmoll (1991, 1993), however, take important steps integrating these approaches through a more historical and sensuous approach to spirit possession. See also A. Napier (1983).
10. J. Rouch (1989, 339).
11. Ibid., 340.
12. P. Connerton (1989,5).
13. Ibid., 22.
14. See J. Austin (1962).
15. P. Connerton (1989,59).
16. Ibid., 61.
17. Ibid., 71.
18. Ibid., 72.
19. Ibid., 96.
20. See G. Lipsitz (1990); see also R. Terdiman (1985).
21. J. Boddy (1989).
22. T. Morrison (1987b, 119).
23. See M. Henderson (1991).
24. G. Jones (1986,22).
25. Ibid., 101–2.
26. J-P Olivier de Sardan (1982, 1984).

27. M. es-Saadi (1900); M. Kati (1911).

28. See T. Hale (1990). For a parallel case material on Greek and Balinese epics, see A. Napier (1992).

29. J-P Olivier de Sardan (1976, 1982).

30. M. Taussig (1993,2).

31. Ibid., 8.

32. Ibid., 8.

33. Ibid., 8.

34. Ibid., 19.

35. See M. Jackson (1989); P. Stoller (1989b, 1992, 1995).

36. M. Taussig (1993,39).

37. H. Cole (1982).

38. M. Taussig (1993,247).

39. Ibid., 242.

40. Ibid., 242.

Chapter 4: "Conscious" Ain't Consciousness

1. G. Jones (1986,103).

2. S. Buck-Morss (1994).

3. S. Eisenstein (1975).

4. See L. Mulvey (1975 [1985]); T. De Lauretis (1984); C. Penley (1989); T. De Lauretis (1987); C. Metz (1971); I. Hedges (1991).

5. See M. Taussig (1993); S. Buck-Morss (1989).

6. S. Buck-Morss (1994, 45). See also A. Napier (1992) on Husserl.

7. S. Buck-Morss (1994, 45). And yet Napier (personal communication) writes: "Cinema is one of the least canonically flexible media; we can listen to music all day without understanding a word, but try showing a film with an unintelligible sound track and people are outraged. What is physical about the cinema? *Double Theatre*, my new video, is very hard to listen to because more than one person is speaking most of the time. I can see people suffer (as they should) when they view it. But "goodness" in cinema is largely reserved for films that reinforce laziness. I think the medium has cathartic potential, but I don't think it is necessarily cathartic—at least in its current state."

8. Ibid., 47.

9. Ibid., 48.

10. See P. Virilio (1989).

11. See L. Williams (1981); P. Stoller (1992).

12. S. Buck-Morss (1994,56).

13. See P. Stoller (1992).

14. See R. Morris (1996).

15. J. Frykman (1994).

16. Ibid., 82.

17. Ibid., 78.

18. Ibid., 82.

19. S. Buck Morss(1994, 55).
20. A. Feldman (1994).
21. Ibid., 89.
22. Ibid., 90.
23. See D. Lowe (1982); J. Crary (1991).
24. See R. Coombe, in press.
25. Ibid., 92.
26. See C. Miller (1985); P. Stoller (1992).
27. A. Feldman (1994,104).
28. Ibid., 88.
29. Ibid., 89.
30. C. Seremetakis (1994).
31. Ibid., 23.
32. Ibid., 26.
33. Ibid., 29.
34. Ibid., 37.
35. Ibid., 37.
36. Ibid., 38.

Part Three: Introduction

1. K. Hastrup (1994,237).
2. R. Shweder (1991,11).
3. K. Hastrup (1994,237).

Chapter 5: Spaces, Places, and Fields

1. G. Clark (1994,186–88); P. Bohannan (1962).
2. See I. Lewis (1980,15–19); E. Grégoire (1993,107).
3. See S. Amin (1971); J. Gugler and W. Flanagan (1978).
4. See J. Rouch (1956); T. Painter (1988); P. Stoller (1992).
5. See L. Brenner (1993). The Quadriya, Tijaniya, Hammalliya, and Muridiya all represent important Sufi brotherhoods in West Africa. The Wahabis are anti-mystical and reject Sufi practices. Differences among all these sects have prompted political schism and turmoil in West Africa. The Mourids are an important political force in contemporary Senegal. Their transnational economic networks have become increasingly important in Europe and in New York City. See also V. Ebin (1990). For more detailed information on the Mourids, see C. O'Brien (1971) and note 15 below.
6. E. Grégoire (1993,113).
7. Indeed, on July 8, 1994 a major ring of video pirates was "busted" in White Plains, but this did not disrupt the supply of pirated videos on 125th Street; see *New York Times* (1994a, B8). Whether the New York mafia actually is involved in video pirating is an open question.

8. Interview with Amadou Adamou, December 17, 1994.

9. See C. Steiner (1993); L. Taylor, I. Barbash, and C. Steiner (1992).

10. See J. Rouch (1956).

11. Economic anthropologists have been describing trading networks and market systems for decades, detailing and analyzing various exchange discourses. See Polanyi's classic *The Great Transformation* (1957) as well as the detailed market descriptions of *Malinowski in Mexico* (1982). This chapter has been about the symbolic and political ramifications of spatial practices in one market. In future publications I hope to describe the dynamics of buying and selling in several of New York City's transnational markets.

12. See Bluestone (1991); McCay (1940); Osofsky (1971); Thomas (1995).

13. Interview with Siddo Seyni, July 15, 1993.

14. V. Ebin and R. Lake (1992); R. Coombe and P. Stoller (1994).

15. See V. Ebin and R. Lake (1992); R. Coombe and P. Stoller (1994). The Mourids, a Sufi brotherhood headquartered in Touba City, Senegal, were founded by Cheik Ahamadou Bamba in 1898. French colonial officials found the brotherhood a threat to the established order and expelled Ahamadou Bamba from Senegal. During his exile the size of the brotherhood swelled and it is today a major political and economic force in Senegal. An offshoot of the Tijani brotherhood, Mouridism stresses that the pathway to salvation is through hard work and trade. Accordingly, the brotherhood acquired vast tracts of land used for groundnut cultivation, and sent its devotees overseas—to France and the United States—to earn hard currency. For more detailed information see C. O'Brien (1971).

16. Interview with Amadou Adamou, October 15, 1994.

17. Interview with Salif Maiga, July 18, 1993.

18. Files of the author.

19. Interview with Issifi Harouna, July 18, 1993, who also suggested that Dinkins, being a black man, would be afraid to adopt a policy that would incite racial conflict. When he announced his plan to disband the 125th Street Market in 1992, Mayor Dinkins revealed that as a youth in Harlem he, too, had been a peddler. See D. Sontag (1993).

20. M. Kaufman (1993).

21. M. Castells and A. Portes (1989,12).

22. R. Coombe and P. Stoller (1994,253–54); see also S. Sassen (1991).

23. J. Hicks (1994a,42).

24. Ibid.

25. Interview with Amadou Adamou, August 19, 1994. Indeed, economic activity along 116th and Lenox is depressed, due in part to the presence of many burned out buildings and the absence of commercial establishments.

26. Interview with Abdou Karimoun and Issifi Harouna, August 19, 1994.

27. Interview with Amadou Adamou, August 19, 1994.

28. The key political groups supporting the mayoral crackdown constitute the Harlem business and political establishment. They include Community Board #10, the local governing council of central Harlem and its chairwoman Barbara Askins, who is also executive director of the 125th Street Business Improvement District (BID); the Harlem Urban Development Corporation, which was set up in 1971 by Governor Nelson Rockefeller to attract commercial development and spur new housing in depressed areas of Harlem; and nearly all Harlem's city and state elected officials. Even though the Masjid Malcolm Shabazz, established after Malcolm X's disassociation from the Nation of Islam, is not part of the Harlem business and political establishment, it too supported the mayoral crackdown. The Masjid stresses fidelity to Sunni Islam. Headed by devotees of Malcolm Shabazz, they, as landlords, stood to profit substantially from the move of the market to 116th Street. Those opposed to Giuliani's decision included the loosely organized 125th Street Vendors Association, which came into existence when Mayor Dinkins attempted to shut down the Harlem market in 1992. Headed by Morris Powell, who has been a street vendor in Harlem for more than thirty years, the Association's estimated membership of 500 vendors consists mostly of African American merchants, but there is also a contingent of West Africans. Members are asked to pay a fee of $20 a month to finance a newsletter and promote peddling. Powell has long been an advocate of the self-determination of black people in Harlem and has long been at odds with the Harlem business and political establishment. Powell's organization was supported by the Nation of Islam, which also supports African American self-determination in Harlem. Such self-determination is also a theme espoused by the Reverend Al Sharpton, who has unsuccessfully run for political office in New York State. For more detailed information on Morris Powell, see D. Barry and J. Hicks (1995). One could say that social class seems to be a significant political determinant in this case. For other analysis of the African market's demise see D. Thomas (1995) and S. Zukin (1995,230–47).

29. Files of the author.

30. Interview with Issifi Harouna, October 15, 1994.

31. Interview with Soulay Younoussa, October 15, 1994.

32. J. Hicks (1994b); interviews with Abdou Karimoun and Issifi Harouna, October 15, 1994.

33. Interview with Chaibou Anzuru, October 15, 1994.

34. J. Hicks (1994b, B3).

35. C. Policano (1994a, 2).

36. Ibid., 2.

37. Ibid., 2.

38. Interview with Amadou Adamou, October 15, 1994.

39. C. Policano (1994b, 9).

40. Ibid., 9.

41. Interview with Issifi Harouna, October 17, 1994.

42. E. Shipp (1994,15).
43. A. Sinclair (1994,28).
44. A. Finder (1994),B1).
45. Editorial, *New York Times* October 21, 1994,21.
46. C. Lévi-Strauss (1967).
47. A. Gupta and J. Ferguson (1992,7).
48. Ibid., 9.
49. See D. Harvey (1989).
50. See R. Coombe and P. Stoller (1994).
51. See A. Gupta and J. Ferguson (1992,17); see also M. Merleau-Ponty (1962) and P. Stoller (1989b).
52. See N. Glick-Shiller, L. Basch and C. Szanton (1992).
53. M. Watts (1992, 126).

Chapter 6: Artaud, Rouch, and the Cinema of Cruelty

1. This scenario is reproduced from N. Echard and J. Rouch (1988).
2. A. Bermel (1977, 113–19).
3. See R. Kuenzli (1987); L. Williams (1981).
4. L. Williams (1981).
5. Ibid., 20.
6. Ibid., 21–22.
7. Williams's semiotic and psychoanalytic analysis of Surrealist film is an important contribution. Contrary to the uncritical analysis of the Surrealism and the cinema that proceeded her work, Williams suggests that Surrealist films "are about the signifying processes of desire in the human subject." Her careful frame by frame analysis of *Un chien andalou* is revelatory and demonstrates how Surrealist filmmakers used formal cinematic devices to promote their revolutionary ends.
8. A. Artaud (1958,84).
9. See S. Buck-Morss (1994); A. Feldman (1994).
10. A. Artaud (1958,74).
11. Ibid.
12. Tyler (1987) makes a similar point in his analysis of Paul Friedrich's poetry, some fifty years after the initial publication of Artaud's manifesto.
13. A. Artaud (1958,79).
14. There is a voluminous literature on the relation of ritual and art, especially in the classics. See A. Napier (1986) and especially (1992) on Bernini's "Double Theatre."
15. A. Napier (1992, 91).
16. See A. Breton (1929); L. Lippard (1970); A. Balakian (1986); J. Clifford (1988); and M. Richman (1990).
17. A. Bermel (1977,40).
18. G. Rouget (1980); see also A. Napier (1986, 1992).
19. A. Schaeffner (1965); M. Leiris (1958); J-M Gibbal (1988).
20. Influenced by Aristotle's writings on trance in the *Politics*, a group

of French scholars consider possession as a kind of cultural theater (see A. Schaeffner 1965, M. Leiris 1958, and G. Rouget 1980) This hypothesis is a highly attractive one, but my own suspicion is that while spirit possession is doubtless a dramatic form, one cannot reduce such a complex phenomenon to "drama" or "theater" (see Stoller 1989a). The great majority of Rouch's films are about Songhay possession ceremonies, a ritual that has fascinated him since 1942 when he witnessed his first ceremony in Gangell, Niger.

21. L. Williams (1981).
22. See A. Schaeffner (1965).
23. N. Echard and J. Rouch (1988); P. Stoller (1992).
24. R. Bensmaia, quoted in R. Predal (1982,55).
25. M. de Montaigne (1948, 152).
26. Trinh T. Minh-ha (1992,86).
27. J. Homiak (1991).
28. J. Rouch and E. Fulchignoni (1989, 299).

Epilogue: Sensuous Ways of Knowing/Living

1. Adapted from I. Shah (1970,84–85).
2. E. Jabès (1993, 29).

WORKS CITED

Amin, Samar, ed. 1974. *Modern Migrations in Western Africa.* Eleventh International African Seminar, 1978. London: Oxford University Press.

Artaud, Antonin 1958. *The Theater and Its Double,* trans. Mary Caroline Richards. New York: Grove Press.

Austin, J. L. 1962. *How To Do Things with Words.* Cambridge, Mass.: Harvard University Press.

Balakian, Anna. E. [1970] 1986. *Surrealism: The Road to the Absolute.* Chicago: University of Chicago Press.

Barry, Dan and Jonathan P. Hicks. 1995. Protestor Is Caught in Fatal Fire's Glare: New Look at Harsh Message. *New York Times,* December 15: B1, B4.

Barthes, Roland. 1972. To Write: An Intransitive Verb. In *The Structuralists: From Marx to Lévi-Strauss,* ed. Richard T. De George and Fernande M. De George. Pp. 164–72. Garden City, N.Y.: Doubleday.

———. 1977. *Image-Music-Text.* Trans. Stephen Heath. New York: Hill and Wang.

Bauman, Zygmunt. 1992. *Intimations of Postmodernity.* London: Routledge.

Beattie, John and John Middleton, eds. 1969. *Spirit Mediumship and Society in Africa.* London: Routledge and Kegan Paul.

Beidelman, Thomas O. 1989. Review of James Clifford's *The Predicament of Culture. Anthropos* 84: 263–67.

Bergé, Christine. n.d. De l'autre côte du miroir. Files of the author.

Bermel, Albert. 1977. *Artaud's Theatre of Cruelty.* New York: Taplinger Publishing Company.

Bird, Charles. 1971. Oral Art in the Mande. In *Papers on the Mandinge,* ed. C. T. Hodge. Pp. 15–27. Bloomington: Indiana University Press.

Birth, Kevin. 1990. Reading and the Righting of Writing Ethnographies. *American Ethnologist* 17: 549–58.

Bluestone, Daniel. 1991. The Pushcart Evil: Peddlers, Merchants and New York City's Streets, 1880–1940. *Journal of Urban History* 18(1): 68–92.

Boddy, Janice Patricia. 1989. *Wombs and Alien Spirits: Women, Men, and the Zar Cult in Northern Sudan.* Madison: University of Wisconsin Press.

Bohannon, Paul and George Dalton, eds. 1962. *Markets in Africa.* Evanston, Ill.: Northwestern University Press.

Bordo, Susan. 1987. *The Flight to Objectivity: Essays on Cartesianism and Culture.* Albany, N.Y.: SUNY Press.

Bourdieu, Pierre. 1984. *Distinction: A Social Critique of the Judgement of Taste*. Cambridge, Mass.: Harvard University Press.

Bourguignon, Erica. 1976. *Possession*. San Francisco: Chandler.

Bowles, Paul. 1976. *The Sheltering Sky*. New York: New Directions.

Brenner, Louis, ed. 1993. *Muslim Identity and Social Change in Sub-Saharan Africa*. Bloomington: Indiana University Press.

Breton, André. 1929. *Manifestes du Surréalisme*. Paris: Kra.

Buck-Morss, Susan. 1989. *The Dialectics of Seeing: Walter Benjamin and the Arcades Project*. Cambridge, Mass.: MIT Press.

————. 1994. The Cinema Screen as Prosthesis of Perception: A Historical Account. In *The Senses Still: Perception and Memory as Material Culture*, ed. C. Nadia Seremetakis. Pp. 45–63. Boulder, Co: Westview Press.

Butler, Judith. 1990. *Gender Trouble: Feminism and the Subversion of Identity*. New York: Routledge.

Camara, Sory. 1976. *Gens de la parole: essai sur la condition et la rôle des griots dans la société Malinke*. The Hague: Mouton.

Carrithers, Michael. 1990. Is Anthropology Art or Science? *Current Anthropology* 31: 263–83.

Castells, Manuel and Alejandro Portes. 1989. The World Underneath. In *The Informal Economy: Studies in Advanced and Less Developed Countries*, ed. Alejandro Portes, Manuel Castells, and Lauren Benton. Pp. 11–37. Baltimore: Johns Hopkins University Press.

Cesara, Manda. 1981. *Reflections of a Woman Anthropologist: No Hiding Place*. New York: Academic Press.

Chernoff, John. 1979. *African Rhythm and African Sensibility: Aesthetics and Social Action in African Musical Idioms*. Chicago: University of Chicago Press.

————. n.d. *A Drummer's Testament*. Chicago: University of Chicago Press. Forthcoming.

Cixous, Hélène. 1976. The Laugh of Medusa (K. and P. Cohen, trans.) *Signs* 1(4): 875–93.

Clark, Gracia. 1994. *Onions Are My Husband: Survival and Accumulation by West African Market Women*. Chicago: University of Chicago Press.

Classen, Candace. 1993. *Worlds of Sense: Exploring the Senses in History and Across Cultures*. New York: Routledge.

Clastres, Pierre. 1974. *La société contre l'état: Recherches d'anthropologie politique*. Paris: Editions de Minuit.

Clifford, James. 1988. *The Predicament of Culture: Twentieth-Century Ethnography, Literature, and Art*. Cambridge, Mass.: Harvard University Press.

Clifford, James and George E. Marcus, eds. 1986. *Writing Culture: The Poetics and Politics of Ethnography*. Berkeley: University of California Press.

Cole, Herbert. 1982. *Mbari: Art and Life Among the Owerri Igbo*. Bloomington: Indiana University Press.

Comaroff, Jean. 1985. *Body of Power, Spirit of Resistance: The Culture and History of a South African People*. Chicago: University of Chicago Press.

Connerton, Paul. 1989. *How Societies Remember.* Cambridge: Cambridge University Press.

Coombe, Rosemary J. 1991a. Encountering the Postmodern: New Directions in Cultural Anthropology. *Canadian Review of Sociology and Anthropology* 28: 188–205.

———. 1991b. Beyond Modernity's Meanings: Engaging the Postmodern in Cultural Anthropology. *Culture* 11(1–2): 97–111.

———. In press. *Cultural Appropriations: Intellectual Property Laws, Postmodern Culture, and Late Modern Politics.* London: Routledge, forthcoming.

Coombe, Rosemary J. and Paul Stoller. 1994. X Marks the Spot: The Ambiguities of African Trading in the Commerce of the Black Public Sphere. *Public Culture* 7(1): 249–75.

Crapanzano, Vincent. 1973. *The Hamshada: A Study in Moroccan Ethnography.* Berkeley: University of California Press.

———. 1980. *Tuhami: Portrait of a Moroccan.* Chicago: University of Chicago Press.

Crary, Jonathan. 1991. *Techniques of the Observer: On Vision and Modernity in the Nineteenth Century.* Cambridge, Mass.: MIT Press.

De Lauretis, Teresa. 1984. *Alice Doesn't: Feminism, Semiotics, Cinema.* Bloomington: Indiana University Press.

———. 1987. *Technologies of Gender: Essays on Theory, Film, and Fiction.* Bloomington: Indiana University Press.

Deleuze, Gilles. 1986. *Cinema 1: The Movement-Image,* trans. Hugh Tomlinson and Barbara Habberjam. Minneapolis: University of Minnesota Press.

———. 1989. *Cinema 2: The Time Image,* trans. Hugh Tomlinson and Robert Goleta. Minneapolis: University of Minnesota Press.

Desjarlais, Robert. 1992. *Body and Emotion: The Aesthetics of Illness and Healing in the Nepal Himalayas.* Philadelphia: University of Pennsylvania Press.

Devereux, Georges. 1967. *From Anxiety to Method in the Behavioral Sciences.* The Hague: Mouton.

Douglas, Mary T., ed. 1970. *Witchcraft Confessions and Accusations.* London: Tavistock.

Dumont, Jean-Paul. [1978]1992. *The Headman and I: Ambiguity and Ambivalence in the fieldworking Experience.* Prospect Heights, Ill.: Waveland Press.

Dwyer, Kevin. [1982]1991. *Moroccan Dialogues: Anthropology in Question.* Prospect Heights, Ill.: Waveland Press.

Ebin, Victoria. 1990. Commercants et missionnaires: une confrérie Musulmane Sénégalaise à New York. *Hommes et Migrations* 1132: 25–31.

Ebin, Victoria and Rose Lake. 1992. Camelots à New York: les pionniers de l'immigration Sénégalaise. *Hommes et Migrations* 1160: 32–37.

Echard, Nicole and Jean Rouch. 1988. Entretien avec Jean Rouch. A Voix Nu. Entretien d'hier à aujourd'hui. Ten-hour discussion broadcast in July of 1988 on Radio France Culture.

Eisenstein, Sergei. 1975. *The Film Sense,* trans. Jay Leyda. New York: Harcourt, Brace, Jovanovich.

Es-Saadi, Mohammed. 1900. *Tarikh es-Soudan.* Paris: Maisonneuve.

Evans-Pritchard, E. E. 1976. *Witchcraft, Oracles, and Magic Among the Azande.* Oxford: Clarendon Press.

Fabian, Johannes. 1990. *Power and Performance: Ethnographic Explorations Through Proverbial Wisdom and Theater in Shaba, Zaire.* Madison: University of Wisconsin Press.

Featherstone, Mike, Mike Hepworth, and Bryan Turner, eds. 1991. *The Body: Social Process and Cultural Theory.* San Francisco: Sage.

Feldman, Alan. 1994. From Desert Storm to Rodney King via ex-Yugoslavia: On Cultural Anaesthesia. In *The Senses Still: Perception and Memory as Material Culture in Modernity,* ed. C. Nadia Seremetakis. Pp. 87–109. Boulder, CO.: Westview Press. Pp. 87–109.

Fernandez, James W. 1982. *Bwiti: An Ethnography of the Religious Imagination in Africa.* Princeton, N.J.: Princeton University Press.

Finder, Alan. 1994. Bratton Joins Watch over Harlem Boycott. *New York Times,* October 21, p. B1.

Foley, Douglas. 1990. *Learning Capitalist Culture: Deep in the Heart of Tejas.* Philadelphia: University of Pennsylvania Press.

———. 1995. *The Heartland Chronicles.* Philadelphia: University of Pennsylvania Press.

Foucault, Michel. 1970. *The Order of Things: An Archaeology of the Human Sciences.* New York: Random House.

———. 1972. *The Archaeology of Knowledge and the Discourse on Language.* London: Tavistock.

Fox, Richard. 1991. Introduction: Working in the Present. In *Recapturing Anthropology: Working in the Present,* ed. Richard Fox. Pp. 1–17. Santa Fe, N.M.: School of American Research Press.

Frykman, Jonas. 1994. On the Move: The Struggle for the Body in Sweden in the 1930's. In *The Senses Still: Perception and Memory as Material Culture in Modernity,* ed. C. Nadia Seremetakis. Pp. 63–87. Boulder, CO.: Westview Press.

Fugelstad, Finn. 1975. Les Hauka: une interpretation historique. *Cahiers d'Etudes Africaines* 58: 203–16.

———. 1983. *A History of Niger, 1850–1960.* Cambridge: Cambridge University Press.

Geertz, Clifford. 1988. *Works and Lives: The Anthropologist as Author.* Stanford, Ca.: Stanford University Press.

Gergen, Kenneth. 1991. *The Saturated Self: Dilemmas of Identity in Contemporary Life.* New York: Basic Books.

Gibbal, Jean-Marie. 1993. *Genii of the River Niger,* trans. Beth G. Raps. Chicago: University of Chicago Press.

Ginsburg, Faye. 1991. Indigenous Media: Faustian Contract or Global Village? *Cultural Anthropology* 6(1): 92–111.

Glick-Shiller, Nina, Linda Basch, and Christina Szanton. 1992. Transnationalism: A New Analytical Framework for Understanding Migration. *Annals of the New York Academy of Science* 645: 1–45.

Grégoire, Emmanuel. 1993. Islam and the Identity of Merchants in Maradi (Niger). In *Muslim Identity and Social Change in Sub-Saharan Africa*, ed. Louis Brenner. Pp. 106–16. Bloomington: Indiana University Press.

Gugler, Josef and William Flanagan. 1978. *Urbanization and Social Change in West Africa.* Cambridge: Cambridge University Press.

Gupta, Akhil and James Ferguson. 1992. Beyond "Culture": Space, Identity and the Politics of Difference. *Cultural Anthropology* 7(1): 6–24.

Hale, Thomas A. 1990. *Scribe, Griot and Novelist: Narrative Interpreters of the Songhay Empire.* Gainesville: University of Florida Press.

Hampaté Ba, Amadou. 1981. The Living Tradition. *Methodology and African Prehistory*, ed. Joseph Ki-Zerbo. General History of Africa 1. Pp. 166–206. Paris: UNESCO.

Harvey, David. 1989. *The Condition of Postmodernity: An Enquiry into the Origins of Cultural Change.* London: Blackwell.

Hastrup, Kirsten. 1994. Anthropological Knowledge Incorporated. In *Social Experience and Anthropological Knowledge*, ed. Kirsten Hastrup and Peter Hervik. Pp. 224–40. London: Routledge.

Hedges, Inez. 1991. *Breaking the Frame: Film Language and the Experience of Limits.* Bloomington: Indiana University Press.

Henault, Dorothy Todd. 1991. Video Stories from the Dawn of Time. *Visual Anthropology Review* 7(2): 85–101.

Henderson, Mae. 1991. Toni Morrison's *Beloved*: Re-membering the Body as Historical Text. In *Comparative American Identities: Race, Sex, and Nationality in the Modern Text*, ed. H. J. Spillers. Pp. 62–87. New York: Routledge.

Hicks, Jonathan. 1994a. Police Move Illegal Vendors from Harlem Thoroughfare. *New York Times*, October 18, p. B3.

———. 1994b. Vendors' Ouster and Boycott Divide Harlem. *New York Times*, October 23, p. 1/43.

Holston, James. 1989. *The Modernist City: An Anthropological Critique of Brasilia.* Chicago: University of Chicago Press.

Homiak, John. 1991. Images on the Edge of the Text. *Wide Angle:*

Howes, David, ed. 1991. *Varieties of Sensory Experience: A Sourcebook in the Anthropology of the Senses.* Toronto: University of Toronto Press.

Husserl, Edmund. 1970. *Logical Investigations.* London: J. N. Findlay.

Irvine, Judith. 1978. When Is Genealogy History? Wolof Genealogies in Comparative Perspective. *American Ethnologist* 5: 651–74.

Jabès, Edmond. 1993. *The Book of Margins*, trans. Rosemary Waldrup. Chicago: University of Chicago Press.

Jackson, Michael. 1986. *Barawa and the Way Birds Fly in the Sky: An Ethnographic Novel.* Washington, D.C.: Smithsonian Institution Press.

———. 1989. *Paths Toward a Clearing: Radical Empiricism and Ethnographic Inquiry.* Bloomington: Indiana University Press.

Jagger, Alison and Susan Bordo, eds. 1989. *Gender/Body/Knowledge: Feminist Reconstructions of Being and Knowing.* New Brunswick, N.J.: Rutgers University Press.

Jones, Gayl. [1975] 1986. *Corregidora.* Boston: Beacon Press.

Kati, Mahmoud. 1911. *Tarikh al Fattach.* Paris: Maisonneuve.

Kaufman, Michael T. 1993. Squeegees and Hope: New Peril. Men Who Wash Car Windows on Street Targeted by William J. Bratton. *New York Times,* December 8, A18, B5.

Kehoe, Alice and Dody H. Giletti. 1981. Women's Preponderance in Possession Cults: The Calcium-Deficiency Hypothesis Extended. *American Anthropologist* 83: 549–62.

Kilbride, Philip and Janet Capriotti Kilbride. 1990. *Changing Family Life in East Africa: Women and Children at Risk.* University Park: Pennsylvania State University Press.

Kondo, Dorrine. 1990. *Crafting Selves: Power, Gender, and Discourses of Identity in a Japanese Workplace.* Chicago: University of Chicago Press.

Kristeva, Julia. 1980. *Desire in Language: A Semiotic Approach to Literature and Art.* New York: Columbia University Press.

———. 1984. *Revolution in Poetic Language.* New York: Columbia University Press.

Kuenzli, Rudolph, ed. 1987. *Dada and Surrealist Film.* New York: Willis, Locker and Owens.

Lambek, Michael. 1981. *Human Spirits: A Cultural Account of Trance in Mayotte.* Cambridge: Cambridge University Press.

Lan, David. 1985. *Guns and Rain: Guerrillas and Spirit Mediums in Zimbabwe.* Berkeley: University of California Press.

Leiris, Michel [1958] 1980. *La possession et ses aspects théatraux chez les Ethiopiens de Gondar.* Paris: Le Sycomore.

Lett, James. 1991. Interpretive Anthropology, Metaphysics and the Paranormal. *Journal of Anthropological Research* 47: 305–29.

Lévi-Strauss, Claude. 1956. *Tristes tropiques.* Paris: Plon.

———. 1967. *Structural Anthropology.* Garden City, N.Y.: Doubleday.

———. 1982. *The Way of Masks.* Seattle: University of Washington Press.

———. 1988. *De près et de loin.* Paris: Editions Odile Jacob.

Lewis, I. M. 1971. *Ecstatic Religion: An Anthropological Study of Spirit Possession.* Harmondsworth: Penguin.

———, ed. 1980. *Islam in Tropical Africa.* Bloomington: Indiana University Press.

Lippard, Lucy. 1970. *Surrealists on Art.* Englewood Cliffs, N.J.: Prentice-Hall.

Lipsitz, George. 1990. *Time Passages: Collective Memory and American Popular Culture.* Minneapolis: University of Minnesota Press.

Lowe, Donald M. 1982. *History of Bourgeois Perception.* Chicago: University of Chicago Press.

MacDougall, David. 1992. Films of Memory. *Visual Anthropology Review* 8(1): 29–38.

Malinowski, Bronislaw and Julio de la Fuente. 1982. *Malinowski in Mexico: The Economics of a Mexican Market System.* London: Routledge and Kegan Paul.

Manganaro, Marc, ed. 1990. *Modernist Anthropology: From Fieldwork to Text.* Princeton, N.J.: Princeton University Press.

Marcus, George E. 1990. The Modernist Sensibility in Recent Ethnographic Writing and the Cinematic Metaphor of Montage. *Visual Anthropology Review* 6(1): 2–12.

Marcus, George E. and Dick Cushman. 1982. Ethnographies as Texts. *Annual Reviews of Anthropology* 11: 25–69.

Marcus, George E. and Michael M. F. Fischer. 1985. *Anthropology as Cultural Critique: An Experimental Moment in the Human Sciences.* Chicago: University of Chicago Press.

Martin, Emily. 1987. *The Woman in the Body: A Cultural Analysis of Reproduction.* Boston: Beacon Press.

Marwick, Max. 1952. The Social Context of Cewa Witch Beliefs. *Africa* 22: 120–35, 215–53.

Masquelier, Adeline. 1993. Narratives of Power, Images of Wealth: The Ritual Economy of Bori in the Market. In *Modernity and Its Malcontents: Ritual and Power in Postcolonial Africa,* ed. Jean Comaroff and John Comaroff. Chicago: University of Chicago Press. Pp. 3–34.

———. 1995. Consumption, Prostitution, and Reproduction: The Poetics of Sweetness in Bori. *American Ethnologist* 22(4): 883–907.

McCay, Claude. 1940. *Harlem: Negro Metropolis.* New York: Dutton.

Merleau-Ponty, Maurice. 1962. *The Phenomenology of Perception.* London: Routledge and Kegan Paul.

———. 1964. *Signs.* Evanston, Ill.: Northwestern University Press.

Metz, Christian. 1971. *Langage et cinéma.* Paris: Larousse.

Middleton, John and Edward H. Winter, eds. 1963. *Witchcraft and Sorcery in East Africa.* New York: Praeger.

Miller, Christopher. 1985. *Blank Darkness: Africanist Discourse in French.* Chicago: University of Chicago Press.

———. 1990. *Theories of Africans: Francophone Literature and Anthropology in Africa.* Chicago: University of Chicago Press.

Mitchell, Timothy. 1988. *Colonizing Egypt.* Berkeley: University of California Press.

Monfouga-Nicholas, Jacqueline. 1972. *Ambivalence et culte de possession.* Paris: Editions Anthropos.

Montaigne, Michel de. 1948. *The Complete Essays of Montaigne.* Palo Alto, Ca.: Stanford University Press.

Morrison, Toni. 1987a. *Beloved.* New York: Knopf.

———. 1987b. The Site of the Truth. In *Inventing the Truth: The Art and Craft of Memoir,* ed. William Zinsser. Boston: Houghton Mifflin. Pp. 109–32.

Morris, Rosalind C. 1996. Anthropology in the Body Shop: *Lords of the Garden,* Cannibalism, and the Consuming Desire of Televisual Anthropology. *American Anthropologist* 98(1): 137–46.

Mudimbe, Valentin Y. 1988. *The Invention of Africa: Gnosis, Philosophy and the Order of Knowledge.* Bloomington: Indiana University Press.

Muller, Jean-Claude. 1971. Review of *Les maîtres fous. American Anthropologist* 73: 1471–73.

Mulvey, Laura. [1975] 1985. Visual Pleasure and Narrative Cinema. In

Movies and Methods II, ed. Bill Nichols. Berkeley: University of California Press.

Napier, A. David. 1986. *Masks, Transformations, and Paradox.* Berkeley: University of California Press.

———. 1992. *Foreign Bodies: Performance, Art, and Symbolic Anthropology.* Berkeley: University of California Press.

Narayan, Kirin. 1989. *Storytellers, Saints, and Scoundrels: Folk Narrative and Hindu Religious Teaching.* Philadelphia: University of Pennsylvania Press.

N'Diaye, Boubacar. 1970. *Les castes au Mali.* Bamako: Editions Populaires.

New York Times. 1994a. Video Ring Is Broken, Police Say. July 8, pp. B3, B8.

———. 1994b. Walking on 125th Street. Editorial. October 21, p. 21.

Obeysekere, Gananath. 1981. *Medusa's Hair: An Essay on Personal Symbols and Religious Experience.* Chicago: University of Chicago Press.

O'Brien, Conor Cruise. 1971. *The Mourids.* Oxford: Clarendon Press.

Olivier de Sardan, Jean-Pierre. 1976. *Quand nos pères étaient captifs.* Paris: Nubia.

———. 1982. *Concepts et conceptions Sonay-Zarma.* Paris: Nubia.

———. 1984. *Sociétés Sonay-Zarma.* Paris: Karthala.

———. 1993. La surinterpretation politique: le culte de possession Hawka du Niger. In *Religion et modernité politique en Afrique noire,* ed. Jean-Francois Bayart. Pp. 163–213. Paris: Karthala.

Osofsky, Gilbert. 1971. *Harlem, the Making of a Ghetto: A History of Negro New York, 1900–1920.* New York: Harper and Row.

Painter, Thomas. 1988. From Warriors to Migrants: Critical Perspectives on Early Migrations Among the Zarma of Niger. *Africa* 58(1): 87–100.

Penley, Constance. 1989. *The Future of an Illusion: Film, Feminism, and Psychoanalysis.* Minneapolis: University of Minnesota Press.

Polanyi, Karl. 1957. *The Great Transformation: The Political and Economic Origins of Our Time.* Boston: Beacon Press.

Policano, Christopher. 1994a. Showdown Today on Rudy Plan to Evict Harlem Vendors. *New York Post,* October 17, p. 2.

———. 1994b. 22 Busted in Melee At Vendors' March. *New York Post,* October 18, p. 9.

Predal, René, ed. 1982. *Jean Rouch, un griot Gallois.* Special issue of *CinemAction* 17. Paris: Harmattan.

Price, Richard. 1983. *First Time.* Baltimore: Johns Hopkins University Press.

Rabinow, Paul. 1985. Discourse and Power: On the Limits of Ethnographic Texts. *Dialectical Anthropology* 10 (1–2): 1–15.

———. 1989. *French Modern.* Cambridge, Mass.: MIT Press.

Richman, Michelle. 1990. Anthropology and Modernism in France: From Durkheim to the Collège de Sociologie. In *Modernist Anthropology: From Fieldwork to Text,* ed. Marc Manganaro. Pp. 183–215. Princeton, N.J.: Princeton University Press.

Riesman, Paul. 1977. *Freedom in Fulani Social Life.* Chicago: University of Chicago Press.

Rorty, Richard. 1979. *Philosophy and the Mirror of Nature.* Princeton, N.J.: Princeton University Press.

———. 1989. *Contingency, Solidarity, and Irony.* Cambridge: Cambridge University Press.

———. 1991. *Objectivity, Relativism, and Truth.* Cambridge: Cambridge University Press.

Rosaldo, Renato. 1989. *Culture and Truth: The Remaking of Social Analysis.* Boston: Beacon Press.

Rose, Dan. 1987. *Black American Street Life: South Philadelphia, 1969–1971.* Philadelphia: University of Pennsylvania Press.

———. 1989. *Patterns of American Culture: Ethnography and Estrangement.* Philadelphia: University of Pennsylvania Press.

Rouch, Jean. 1956. Migrations au Ghana. *Journal de la Société des Africanistes* 26 (1–2): 33–196.

———. 1989a. *La religion et la magie Songhay.* 2nd ed. Brussels: Free University.

———. 1990. Interview. Paris, March 1, 1990.

Rouch, Jean and Enrico Fulchignoni. 1989. Conversation Between Jean Rouch and Professor Enrico Fulchignoni. *Visual Anthropology* 2(2): 265–301.

Rouget, Gilbert. 1980. *La musique et la transe.* Paris: Gallimard.

Ruby, Jay. 1991. Speaking For, Speaking About, Speaking With, or Speaking Alongside—The Documentary Dilemma. *Visual Anthropology Review* 7(2): 50–68.

Said, Edward. 1978. *Orientalism.* New York: Random House.

———. 1989. Representing the Colonized: Anthropology's Interlocutors. *Critical Inquiry* 15: 205–25.

Sangren, P. Stephen. 1988. Rhetoric and the Authority of Ethnography. *Current Anthropology* 30(5): 555–69.

Sassen, Saskia. 1991. *The Global City: New York, London, Tokyo.* Princeton, N.J.: Princeton University Press.

Scarry, Elaine. 1986. *The Body in Pain: The Making and Unmaking of the World.* London and New York: Oxford University Press.

Schaeffner, André. 1965. Rituel et pré-théatre. In *Histoire des spectacles: sous la direction de Guy Dumur.* Pp. 21–54. Paris: Gallimard.

Schmoll, Pamela. 1991. *Searching for Health in a World of Disease.* Ph.D. Dissertation. Department of Anthropology, University of Chicago.

Seremetakis, C. Nadia. 1994. The Memory of the Senses, Part II: Still Acts. In *The Senses Still: Perception and Memory as Material Culture in Modernity,* ed. C. Nadia Seremetakis. Pp. 23–45. Boulder, Co.: Westview Press.

Shah, Idreis. 1970. *Tales of the Dervishes.* New York: Dutton.

Shipp, E. R. 1994. Cool It, Face Facts in Harlem. *New York Daily News,* October 19, p. 15.

Shweder, Richard. 1991. *Thinking Through Cultures: Explorations in Cultural Psychology.* Cambridge, Mass.: Harvard University Press.

Sinclair, Abiola. 1994. Boycott of 125th Street? *New York Amsterdam News*, October 15, p. 27.

Soja, Edward. 1989. *Postmodern Geographies: The Reassertion of Space in Critical Social Theory.* London: Verso.

Sontag, Deborah. 1993. To Illegal Street Vendors, American Dream Needs Work, Not License. *New York Times*, June 14, p. A12.

Spivak, Gayatri Chakravorty 1990. *The Postcolonial Critic: Interviews, Strategies, Dialogues.* New York: Routledge.

Starett, Gregory. 1995. The Hexis of Interpretation: Islam and the Body in the Egyptian Popular School. *American Ethnologist* 22(4): 953–70.

Steiner, Christopher. 1993. *African Art in Transit.* Cambridge: Cambridge University Press.

Stoller, Paul. 1989a. *Fusion of the Worlds: An Ethnography of Possession Among the Songhay of Niger.* Chicago: University of Chicago Press.

———. 1989b. *The Taste of Ethnographic Things: The Senses in Anthropology.* Philadelphia: University of Pennsylvania Press.

———. 1992. *The Cinematic Griot: The Ethnography of Jean Rouch.* Chicago: University of Chicago Press.

———. 1995. *Embodying Colonial Memories: Spirit Possession, Power, and the Hauka in West Africa.* New York: Routledge.

Stoller, Paul and Cheryl Olkes. 1987. *In Sorcery's Shadow: A Memoir of Apprenticeship Among the Songhay of Niger.* Chicago: University of Chicago Press.

———. 1990. Sauce épaisse: remarques sur les rapports sociaux chez les Songhay du Niger. *Anthropologie et Sociétés* 14 (3): 57–76.

Suleiman, Susan R. 1986. *The Female Body in Western Culture: Contemporary Perspectives.* Cambridge, Mass.: Harvard University Press.

Taussig, Michael. 1993. *Mimesis and Alterity: A Particular History of the Senses.* New York: Routledge.

Terdiman, Richard. 1985. *Discourse/Counter-Discourse.* Ithaca, N.Y.: Cornell University Press.

Thomas, Deborah. 1995. The Removal of Vendors from Harlem as a Social Drama: Illuminating Economic and Racial Ideologies in an Age of Global Capitalist Restructuring. Unpublished ms.

Trinh T. Minh-ha. 1989. *Woman, Native, Other: Writing Postmodernity and Feminism.* Bloomington: Indiana University Press.

Trinh, T. Minh-ha and Nancy Chen. 1992. Speaking Nearby: A Conversation with Trinh T. Minh-ha. *Visual Anthropology Review* 8(1): 82–91.

Turner, Byran S. 1991. Recent Developments in the Theory of the Body. In *The Body: Social Process and Cultural Theory*, ed. Mike Featherstone, Mike Hepworth and Bryan S. Turner. Pp. 1–36. San Francisco: Sage.

Turner, Terence. 1991. The Kayapo on Television. *Visual Anthropology Review* 8(1): 107–13.

Tyler, Stephen. 1987. *The Unspeakable: Discourse, Dialogue, and Rhetoric in the Post-Modern World.* Madison: University of Wisconsin Press.

Virilio, Paul. 1989. *Cinema and War: The Logistics of Perception.* London: Verso.

Wafer, Jim. 1991. *The Taste of Blood: Spirit Possession in Brazilian Candomble.* Philadelphia: University of Pennsylvania Press.

Watts, Michael. 1992. Space for Everything (A Commentary). *Cultural Anthropology* 7(1): 115–29.

Williams, Linda. 1981. *Forms of Desire: Sexual Orientation and the Social Construction of Controversy.* Berkeley: University of California Press.

Zempleni, Andras. 1968. *L'interpretation et la thérapie traditionelle du desordre mental chez les Wolof et les Lebou (Sénégal).* Paris: Institut d'Ethnologie.

Zukin, Sharon. 1995. *The Cultures of Cities.* Oxford: Blackwell.

FILMS CITED

Bunuel, Luis and Salvador Dali
   1929.   *Un chien andalou.* Paris.
   1931.   *L'âge d'or.* Paris.
Lumière, Louis
   1895.   *L'arrive d'un train à la gâre de Ciotat.* Paris.
Rouch, Jean
   1949.   *Les magiciens de Wanzerbé.* Paris: Comité des Films Ethnogra-
            phiques (CFE).
   1955.   *Les maîtres fous.* Paris: Films de la Pléiade.
   1957.   *Moi, un noir.* Paris: Films de la Pléiade.
   1959.   *La pyramide humaine.* Paris: Films de la Pléiade.
   1960.   *Chronique d'un été.* Paris: Films de la Pléiade.
   1964.   *The Lion Hunters.* Paris: Films de la Pléiade.
   1967.   *Jaguar.* Paris: Films de la Pléiade.
   1969.   *Petit à petit.* Paris: Films de la Pléiade.
Taylor, Lucien, Ilisa Barbash, and Christopher Steiner
   1992.   *In and Out of Africa.* Berkeley: University of California Media
            Extension.

INDEX

Adorno, Theodor, 81
African markets, 96–98; in Harlem, 93, 94, 95, 96–114, 115, 116
Amin, Samir, 149
Artaud, Antonin, xvii–xviii, 53, 75, 77, 92, 120–23, 125, 147n.8; and the cinema, 121–22. *See also* Theater of cruelty
Askia Mohammed Touré, 25, 62
Azande people, 4

Barthes, Roland, 30, 32, 140nn.9–10. *See also* Death of the author
Benjamin, Walter, 66
Berge, Christine, 32, 141nn.18–19, 149. *See also* Implication
Bermal, Albert, 149
Bird, Charles, 27, 140n.3, 149
Boddy, Janice, 42, 59, 139n.8, 142n.5, 149
Body, xi, 3; and memory, 45–87; and politics, 78–80; as written and read, xvi, 5; as text, 5; of the ethnographer, 23; in Sweden, 78–80
Bordo, Susan, 139n.4, 149
Bourdieu, Pierre, xii, 139n.6, 149
Bowles, Paul, 6, 139n.7, 140nn.8–9
Bratton, William, 95, 104, 105, 113, 146n.28
Brenner, Louis, 144n.5, 150
Breton, André, 122, 126, 147n.16, 150
Buck-Morss, Susan, 75–80, 80, 84, 87, 143n.2, 143n.7, 143n.12, 150
Butler, Judith, xiv–xv, 139n.9, 150

Cartesianism, xii, xii, xv, 3. *See also* Bordo; Butler
Chernoff, John M. 28, 140n.7, 150
Cinema, xvii; of cruelty, xviii, 126; as prosthesis, 77–78. *See also* Buck-Morss

Cixous, Hélène, 139n.5, 150. *See also* Écriture féminine
Classen, Constance, 139n.3, 150
Clastres, Pierre, 141n.19, 150
Clifford, James, 140n.12, 141n.31, 150
Colonialism, 53
Conscious, 74–75, 83. *See also* Jones
Commemorative rituals, 58–59, 61. *See also* Connerton
Comaroff, Jean, 150
Connerton, Paul, 57–59, 61, 63, 142n.1, 142nn.12–19, 150
Coombe, Rosemary, 41, 141n.41, 142n.6, 145n.22, 150
Counter-memory, 59. *See also* Lipsitz
Cultural anesthesia, 81. *See also* Buck-Morss; Feldman
Cultural memory, xvi, 45, 65; and embodiment, 45. *See also* Connerton; Feldman; Serematakis

Darwin, Charles, 67, 68
Death-of-the-author, 29–30, 32. *See also* Barthes
Deleuze, Gilles, 76, 151
Desjarlais, Robert, 141n.46, 151
Desnos, Robert, 77, 121
Dinkins, David, 102, 104; administration of 102, 146n.28
Dumont, Jean-Paul, 31, 151

Echard, Nicole, 148n.23, 151
Écriture féminine, 5. *See also* Cixous
Eisenstein, Sergei, 75, 77, 143n.3, 151
Eluard, Paul, 129
Enlightenment, 5
Embodiment, xii, 85; and phenomena, xvi; and sorcery, 22; and ethnography, 26

Epistemology, xvi; western versions, 3; non-western, 3; and griots, 33; and sensuousness, 47

es-Saadi, Mohammed, 62, 143n.27, 151

Ethnofiction, 126–33. *See also* Rouch

Ethnography, 26, 31; and authority, 31; written versions of, 35; filmic versions of, 35; as texts, 39–43. *See also* Marcus; Clifford

Eurocentrism, xiii, xv

Evans-Pritchard, E. E., 4–5, 139n.3, 152

Fabian, Johannes, 152

Farrakhan, Louis, 93, 106, 11, 146n.28

Featherstone, Mike, xiv

Feldman, Allen, 81–83, 84, 86, 87, 144nn.27–29, 147n.9, 152

Feminism, xiii

Ferguson, James, 115

Fernandez, James, 141n.30, 152

First contact, 67–69. *See also* Taussig

Fischer, Michael M. J., 141n.31.,155

Foucault, Michel, xv, 139n.5, 152

Frykman, Jonas, 78–80, 84, 143nn.15–18, 152

Fugelstad, Finn, 53, 152

Geertz, Clifford, 31, 152

Gergen, Kenneth, 40, 141n.36

Giuliani, Rudolph, 94, 104, 105, 146n.28; administration of, 94, 110

Glick-Shiller, Nina, 147n.52, 152

Griaule, Marcel, 119

Griots, 25, 27, 31, 34, 62; in Sahelian West Africa, 26–29; of Songhay, 34; talk of, 35; burdens of, 37; and poetry 38

Gupta, Akhil, 115, 147n.51, 153

Gurmantche people, 68

Halbwachs, Maurice, 58

Hale, Thomas, 140n.1, 153. *See also* Griots

Hampaté Ba, Amadou, 140n.2, 153. *See also* Griots

Harlem, 93, 96–114, 146n.28

Harvey, David, 115, 141n.35, 153. *See also* Postmodernity

Hastrup, Kirsten, 91, 144n.1, 144n.3, 153

Hauka spirits, xvi, xvii, 48–52, 53, 69–73, 120; and embodiment, 55; and second contact, 69–70; roundtables of, 49–52

Hausa people, 97

Heidegger, Martin, xii

Heusch, Luc de, 119

History, 34; and consumption, 34–35; and embodiment, xvi; from below, 45

Holston, James, 42, 141n.44, 153

Homiak, John, 133, 148n.27, 153

Howes, David, 139n.2, 153

Humanists, 91

Humility, 136, 137

Husserl, Edmund, xii, 76, 139n.2, 153

Imaginary signifiers, 122

Implication, 32; and embodiment, 34–36. *See also* Berge

Informal economies, 105

Inscription, 59. *See also* Connerton

Irvine, Judith, 27, 140n.6, 141n.28, 153

Islam, 97–98; and trade, 98

Jabès, Edmond, 136, 148n.2, 153

Jackson, Michael, 22, 140n.14, 142n.8, 153

Jaguar, 36, 120, 126–28, 160. *See also* Rouch

Jenitongo, Adamu, 10–22, 24, 27, 48–52, 70–73

Jones, Gayl, 60–61, 74–75, 142nn.24–25, 143n.1, 153

Kati, Mahmoud, 62, 143n.27, 154

Khadir, xi

Kilbride, Philip, 140n.16, 154

King, Rodney, 82

Kondo, Dorinne, 42, 141n.46, 154

Kuma, 18

Kurumba people, 68
Kuso, 8,9, 13, 72, 73

Lambek, Michael, 142n.5, 154
La pyramide humaine, 120, 129–30, 160. *See also* Rouch
L'âge d'or, 125, 160
L'arrive d'un train dans la gâre de Ciotat, 75, 160
Les magiciens de Wanzerbé, 119, 160
Lévi-Strauss, Claude, 4–5, 86, 114, 127, 128, 139n.1, 147n.46, 154
Les maîtres fous, 53, 119–120, 126. *See also* Rouch
The Lion Hunters, 130, 160. *See also* Rouch
Lipsitz, George, 59, 142n.20, 154

MacDougall, David, 35, 140n.15, 154
Marcus, George, 39, 140n.12, 141n.31, 154
Martin, Emily, xii, 155
Masjid Malcolm Shabazz, 93, 94, 95, 105, 106, 11, 116
Masquelier, Adeline, 155
Memory, xvi; and history, xvi; and the senses, 84–86. *See also* Serematakis
Merleau-Ponty, Maurice, xii, 32, 139n.3, 155
Metz, Christian, 122, 155
Miller, Christopher, 139n.5, 140n.11, 155
Mimesis, xvi, 65–70. *See also* Taussig
Mimetic faculty, 66–67. *See also* Taussig
Mitchell, Timothy, 139n.5, 155
Moi, un noir, 36, 120, 128–29, 160. *See also* Rouch
Montaigne, Michel de, xii, 148n.25, 155
Morris, Rosalind, 143n.14, 155
Morrison, Toni, 60, 142n.22, 155
Mourids, 95, 101. *See also* Sufi; Senegalese
Mudimbe, Valentin, 140n.11, 155

Napier, A. David, 140n.17, 142n.5, 143n.7, 147nn.14–15, 156

Naqshbandi order, xi. *See also* Sufi
Narayan, Kirin, 42, 141n.46, 156
Nation of Islam, 106, 146n.28
New York City, 93–114, 146n.28
Nietzsche, Friedrich, xii

Objectivism, 5
Olivier de Sardan, Jean-Pierre, 142n.26, 143n.29, 156
Operation Desert Storm, 81–83. *See also* Feldman
Oral tradition, 62–63. *See also* Hale; Hampaté Ba

Petit à petit, 36, 120, 130–32, 160. *See also* Rouch
Phallocentrism, xiii
Plato, 84
Postcolonialism, 41
Postmodernism, 30, 32; and ethnography, 40; and postmodernity, 115. *See also* Clifford; Harvey; Marcus
Poststructuralism, xiii, 30. *See also* Foucault
Powell, Morris, 106, 109–14, 146n.28

Rabinow, Paul, 41, 42, 141n.39, 141n.45, 156
Republic of Niger, 8
Riesman, Paul, 31, 157
Romanticism, 9. *See also* Shweder
Rorty, Richard, 3, 139n.1, 157
Rosaldo, Renato, 78, 157
Rose, Dan, 141n.46, 157
Rouch, Jean, xvii–xviii, 25, 27, 35, 42, 53, 56, 78, 92, 119–20, 125, 128, 140n.13, 141n.47, 142nn.10–11, 144n.4, 145n.10, 157, 161; and ethnofiction, 126–33. *See also* Cinema of cruelty; *Les maîtres fous*; Shared anthropology
Rouget, Gilbert, 124, 147n.18, 157
Rumi, x, xviii. *See also* Sufi

Said, Edward, 41, 139n.5, 140n.11, 141n.31, 157
Sambeli, 12–13, 21. *See also* Songhay
Sar, Alioune, 119

Second contact, 69–70. *See also* Taussig
Sembène, Ousmane, 35
Senegalese, 91, 100–102. *See also* Mourid; West African vendors
Sensuousness, xi, xvii
Sensuous scholarship, xv–xviii, 3, 85, 91, 119, 136
Serematakis, C. Nadia, 84–86, 87, 144nn.30–36, 157. *See also* Cultural memory
Shah, Idries, 139n.1, 148n.1, 157
Shared anthropology, 35. *See also* Rouch
Shipp, E. R.,11, 147n.42, 157
Shweder, Richard, 91, 144n.2, 157
Silko, Leslie, 60
Simiri-Sohanci, 16, 17. *See also* Songhay
Sinclair, Abiola, 113, 147n.43, 158
Sohanci, 7. *See also* Jenitongo; Songhay
Sontag, Susan, 128
Squeegee men, 104
Spirit illness, 21. *See also* Spirit possession
Spirit possession, xvi, 38, 55; and the body, 56–57; and cultural memory, 57; and the senses, 55–56; as commemorative ritual, 61
Songhay, 7; and sorcery, 36; elders of, 25–26, 27; empire of, 62; griots of, 25, 34; sorcerers of xvi, xvii, 7, 25. *See also* Jenitongo; Rouch
Steiner, Christopher, 145n.9, 158
Sufi, ix, xi, xvii, 101; stories of x–xi, 135–36. *See also* Rumi; Mourid

Surrealism, 123–25. *See also* Artaud; Breton
Sweden, 78–80. *See also* Frykman

Taussig, Michael, 65–70, 139n.8, 143n.30. *See also* Mimesis
Taylor, Lucien, 161
Text, 54, 63
Theater of cruelty, 53, 122–25. *See also* Artaud
Trinh T. Minh-ha, 132, 148n.26, 158
Tuareg people, 6
Turner, Bryan, xiv, 158
Turner, Victor, 58
Tyler, Stephen, 147n.12, 158

Un chien andalou, 125, 160

Van Sertima, Ivan, 98
Vierya, Paulin, 119
Violence, 81–83; and the theater, 124. *See also* Feldman
Virilio, Paul, 143n.10

Watts, Michael, 147n.53., 159
West Africa, 96, 97; and markets, 98–99
West African vendors, 94, 109, 115; and African Americans in Harlem, 96–114, 115
Williams, Linda, 121–22, 125, 143n.11, 147nn.4–7, 148n.21, 159
Wittgenstein, Ludwig, 91

Zukin, Sharon, 159

Printed in the United States
134898LV00001B/12/A

9 780812 216158